"No Failure"
Introduction
American Dream?

What is the American Dream? It used to be said that the American Dream was home ownership, but that was when everyone worked for large powerful corporations. Today the American Dream is to guide your own ship in this World. To never have to answer to a boss! To provide wealth and glory to your family! To be a mover and a shaker in your neighborhood! What is the new American Dream? It is to open and run your own business.

The dream of owning your own business provides the basis for all of your other dreams too come true. While many Americans try to open their own business most fail. Why do they fail? Why do they see their dreams crash to the ground? Why is their life in ruin? Simply because they have been running their business on "Hopium" which is hoping you will be successful instead of knowing you will be successful. Most people hope that when they put their time and money into realizing their dreams they will be successful. This leads to failure and suffering. Just the hope to run your business in a way to be successful is not enough.

In life we often put more preparation into playing baseball or softball than putting together our plan to be successful. We open businesses with the hope it will be successful. We put our sign up and run an ad. Never truly putting the work into planning the structure of the operation of the business the way we should. When the business fails we say it was the economy or the employees weren't good enough. Rarely do we accept the truth that we did not plan and execute properly. While often we sit around and say when I am successful we will do this or that. We never say what happens if something gets in our way. How do we plan to overcome obstacles on the path to our dreams coming true? If we were to plan for not only success but for things that would normally cause us to fail. We would navigate through tough times by following the road map we should create before we start our journey.

How do we make sure that we will be successful and our Dreams will be realized? That is through not just dreaming and hoping for success, but by planning and holding ourselves accountable for success. What does that mean? What if you wanted to go to Salt Lake City and you lived in Nashville, TN? Would you just jump in a car and start to drive? No you would start to plan. Part of this planning would involve checking the weather conditions along the way and deciding the exact path you will take. You would plan how far you will go each day and what you can spend on the journey. When you start your trip you will look at the gauges in the car to make sure the engine is running fine and you have plenty of gas. If a problem arises you would stop and analysis the situation before you moved forward. After looking at all the options you would make a decision based on your needs and what will help you reach your goal. Then you would start back on your trip after looking at your road map and getting your bearings again.

When we are running a business and something bad happens we often make a quick decision without looking at what would be the best decision to lead us to success. We do not make corrections on our road map. We do not analysis how the problem will affect other areas of our business and what corrections should be made. We just say we will deal with it when another problem arises. The lack of planning could cause the next problem to bankrupt our dreams. Even worse than bankrupting your dreams is that your dream is now a failure and you are caught up in finding a way to bring your failure to a close instead of following the road map you should have followed. In most cases a failed business owner is not bad at the purpose of the business (Car sales, painting, food or what you sold or made) but the business owner could not run the business operation of the business.

The sad thing is that learning the business operation of our business is one of the most important things in getting ready to open a business. But most of us just think that if we can perform our trade that the other stuff will fall in line. That is not reality the other stuff will cause us to fail and end up bankrupt. What if a person was the greatest delivery driver in the world but never learned how to put fuel in their truck? They would never get a chance to show the world how great they were because their truck would never get fueled.

I am writing this book as a road map for people wanting to get into business. So you can start with all the tools necessary for success.

The tools are not hard to learn but they must be not only learned but used. Do not read any farther if you only want to learn about getting the proper gauges for your business but do not plan to use them. Instead return this book and go buy one on "How to Rebuild Your Life after Bankruptcy". The bankruptcy book will be much more useful since you really want to fail. Proper planning will lay the foundation for success no matter what happens in the future. Not planning will lead you down a path laid with credit collectors calling regularly and bankruptcy Court being your destination.

In the following chapters you will find out the steps that need to be taken to plan your businesses future success. We walk through the organizational structure your business should have and what type planning needs to be in place. We will also cover topics such as advertising, accounting, planning for wealth and much more. This book like a well thought out business plan must be used for planning and referred to as you are on your journey to success with your business.

If you are only going to attempt to follow part of this book then please quit reading it now. In order for you to be successful all of the information must be followed. If you feel something does not apply to your circumstances then go through the steps in the book before throwing out the steps. You will find use from all of the things mentioned in this book and all of the different areas must work together like a part in an engine. All the parts of an engine must be there in order for the engine to work properly. If one part is not cared for properly the engine may run but far from maximum efficiency. We want your business to run on all cylinders.

If your business is running with all the gauges and planning it needs you will reach your dream of success. Not because it just happened but because you planned it into being. You want have to hope you will be successful you will know you will be successful. You will have peace of mind and your family will be proud of your success.

So as we move on into the book get your notebook and a pen. Your dreams are about to become reality. Not through the power of hope but through the power of planning and implementation. If you do not want to be successful please do not read on in this book. If you are happy that your dreams constantly get crushed then do not follow what this book teaches you. If you want to be successful and have your business become the powerhouse it can be then read this book.

Before we start put your pen down and close your eyes. Take a series of deep breathes and visualize your dream business. See your success become a reality. Now open your eyes and scream "I will be a Success"!!!!!!!

Now let's start the rest of your life!

Or

Choose Failure and simply close the book!

Chapter 1
What to Do First? What Business Will You Open?

So you want to discover the American dream of owning your own business? What are you going to do first? Some people say you need to start getting financing or you need to start marketing your business. Before anything is done you must design your road map for success.

Why do we jump into business without knowing where we are going? Why are we opening the business? What is our strategy? Where is the money coming from? Where will it open? When will we be successful? When will we be free from fear? When will our dream be realized?

So what is the answer to these questions? Do you really care what the answer is? Well if you don't BANKRUPTCY COURT WILL BE IN YOUR FUTURE! Don't jump into the first business that looks good. Isn't that how many of us choose who we marry and how has that worked? Promise me you will take the time before you run off to fail in business. None of us have to fail if we take the time to survey the future of our business and the direction we want it to go.

So the first thing we need to do in starting a business is to decide what business we want to be in until we reach our goal which is success. Let us first get a piece of paper out and write down what type of businesses we would like to open. Write down what ever you want to do. Look deep into your soul and find what makes your heart excited. What will make your dreams come true? If you like what you do it will make dealing with other issues in running a business much easier.

Now once you have decided on the business you must figure out what skills you need to have to be successful in this business. Let's go through some skills that a business owner might need to be successful. Below is a list of some of the things you must have in your skill set.

Accounting-You are probably thinking of course I know I need to know accounting. Well you need to know more than tax numbers. You need to understand how to keep track of your inventory, materials and much more. Not just how to count them at the end of the month but how to attach a gauge to them so you can watch them daily. Every item on a balance sheet and a Profit and loss statement is an actual living creature. They must be measured and controlled if your business is going to be successful. Gauges must be in place so you can monitor your businesses performance. Do you know how to do this? If you have to think about how many hours you scheduled for yesterday or how much money you have in the bank then you don't. You must master this if you want to be successful. We will cover this in more detail later in the book.

Marketing-What is marketing? Is it advertising? Do you need it? Well marketing should be used as part of your road map we will build at the beginning. Marketing is the overall presentation the customer sees when they do business with you. It is the way your business is laid out, the sales materials you use, the advertising you do, the satisfaction the customer gets from doing business from you and much more. If your marketing plan is well connected to your gauges you will be able to drive your marketing to success. It is not simply advertising? Advertising is useless if it is not part of a plan. If your idea of marketing is to run an ad or send out a mailer then you do not know what effective marketing is so please don't spend a dime till you read the rest of this book.

You're Product-What are you going to sell? Why are you going to sell it? What are your costs in the product? What is your profit margin? Should you be selling this product? This is one of the most important decisions you will ever make besides which Bankruptcy attorney to use if you don't open your mind up and change. All businesses have products whether you are a lawyer or a contractor or even a retailer. You must decide which products to carry. How will you do that? You must decide whether you can make enough profit on the products you to choose to stay in business. You must know every cost associated with your product. The two type costs are variable costs that are directly tired to it as well as your fixed costs which stay the same whether you produce or sell any products. Do you know enough about your product? Are you willing to bet your families future on this product?

Human Resources-Do you know how to hire someone? More importantly do you know when the proper time to add employees is for your business? Are you up to date on EEOC policies? Staffing your company is an important decision. Your staff will represent your company to your customers. A well planned human structure for your business must be installed so that your business has the right human assets to be successful. If planned wrong your hires will set your date with a Bankruptcy Judge. So do not hire on a whim just like all the other parts of your business it must be planned and done with the proper structure.

Negotiating Contracts: Do you sign contracts fast? Are you easy to deal with? Do you hate confrontation? Do you want people to like you? Do you often get the short end of deals? If so you do not negotiate your deals. You sign what people put in front of you. You are hoping that by giving people what they want they might buy you lunch after your Bankruptcy hearing. It does not have to be done this way. The contracts you sign must be in line with your road map. The payments and services that are being performed must be in line for a profit. Whether their being performed on you or if you are doing the performing every aspect of the contract must be examined. From how you are entering into it to how you will get out of it. Remember we never plan on problems occurring but when they do it is better to have planned ahead. So always discuss and have worked out what happens if something falls through. You must always look at every contract or business relationship to ensure your interests are protected.

Organizational Structure Planning-Do you feel flying by the seat of your pants is safer than actually having a plan? Is structure something that is created as you go? If so makes sure you fill out you Bankruptcy papers correct and read all the directions. The Bankruptcy Court does not like sending things back for corrections. The great thing is that you can start today changing your ways and begin organizing your structure. Why do you need structure? Every thing operates better with structure even a business. If you want to achieve profit as an end result then planning a structure that guides revenue through the expense sifter and makes sure there is profit left over. Every part of your organization will work better and in unity with structure and a plan. Do you know how to plan your structure so you will make a profit? Or do you prefer to use "Hopeium" to guide your profit. "Hopeium" is when you hope every thing will go well so you can have a profit. It is better to know you will have a profit instead of hoping you will have a profit.

Sales Structure Planning-Why do you need this? What is this? Why can't you just file bankruptcy and get it over with? Why not just use your life savings you were going to invest in this business to buy Bon Jovi tickets? Why not simply give the money to my wife? Well sales do not just happen except in a poor running organization. You should know where your sales are coming from and when. The sales team should follow your sales plan which is designed to run with the rest of your organization. Your sales plan should focus on selling your most profitable items with the most favorable terms. Do you know how to develop a sales plan? Do you need my wife's address to send you life's savings?

Technical expertise-Can you do the work of the business you are opening? Does this sound crazy? Do you need my wife's address? You do not have to be an artist to own an art gallery or a cabinet maker to own a cabinet shop. You do have to have a plan to hire a competent person to perform the skilled duties. The time to plan and put a strategy in place for success is in before you open.

Wealth Planning-Why are you going to open a business? Do you not plan to make money? What are you going to do with your money? If you don't plan on making money close this book and burn it. Then send all of your future earnings to the IRS or my wife? Just like your business needs a plan you must plan to build wealth with your profit. With proper planning you can make your money work for you. But don't just give your money to someone to handle. What I hope you learn from our conversation through this book is that you need to plan and control all aspects of your life. Decide up front what your expectations are for growth and risk. Then hold them to those expectations.

Now that we have reviewed some of the skills you need to open a business. Now let's look at what skills you have and the ones you need. Go down the list you prepared and the list that I prepared. Take a personal inventory of your skills and decide where you are lacking. Be Honest! Don't say I think I know that well when really you saw a program on it once. There is no shame in not knowing only in failing because of your ego. So make notes on what skills you need and if you have a skill where the limitations may be there. You need to know where your strengths are and where you need help.

What is your next step? What do you think is next? That is right now you go out and obtain those skills before you open your business. By doing this you will be in fighting shape when you open your business and even businesses that have been open for years will be no match for you. Most businesses have no planning and they run on "Hopeium" they will not be prepared to compete against you.

Where do you find these skills if you do not have them already learned or sourced? Where do you hone your skills? Well you could go out and hire people to perform these functions but that is no good because some of these functions you must know how to control. I believe in trying to discover knowledge yourself first then if all else fails then go get help. You need to learn to own these skills and know if you hire someone to perform the duties if they are being done right. Otherwise you might be paying someone to just simply take your money and lead you down a path that does not have a happy ending.

There are many places you can find how to perform these skills. In the following pages I am going to list some resources you can use to learn these skills. Please review the list and decide which of these resources you can use to master these skills.

Local Colleges-Many local colleges or trade schools will have classes covering areas that you need help in. Call all the local schools and get class listings. Then decide which classes would help you if any and call the school and get a more detailed listing of what the class offers.

Internet-The internet is a great resource for any information. Go to a search engine like Yahoo, Google and many more. Type in the subject you need help with and it will search for the answer. You will get many listings simply click on them and read the information. Be careful that you do not purchase information over the web. There is enough out there for free. If you have searched the world over and that is the resource you can find then purchase it.

Consultants-Consultants are a good resource if you can not find the information for free. Remember they are in business to make money. Never tell them how much you have to spend. Only use them as a last resort. Make sure you get references before you hire them and check the better business bureau. We will cover hiring a consultant later in the book.

IRS-The IRS has many great publications to help you learn to handle the tax portion of your business. Do not over look them as a resource. You can go to their local office and they usually have a large selection of brochures. Many offices even have seminars you can attend for free.

Small Business Administration-This is a wonderful resource for information. Many people think they only help you borrow money but they do so much more. They have great seminars on every aspect of your business. They even have an organization of retired executives that will help get your business set up. There is usually no charge for this service. It is like hiring a consultant without the fees. These people really care about making small business successful. If you use them please show your appreciation for their help.

Other Business Owners- If you need help in a certain area and know of a small business person that seems to do a great job at that function. Go to them and ask for them to explain how they do the task. Many will be glad to help a fellow small business person. But be careful don't give all of your plans away especially if they are in the same industry.

Local Government –Many local County and State agencies have programs to help small businesses learn to be successful. In areas of tax and employee relations local governments can be especially helpful.

Libraries-With the advent of the internet many people forget about local libraries but they are a great resource. They have all the information you need some where within their walls. They often have many classes and seminars taught at their facilities.

Now you know the skills you need in the business and you know where to learn to the skills. So it is time to get to work! If you don't feel you are up to the task and would rather just open your business and use 'Hopeium" to guarantee your failure then please close the book. Go and get some coffee maybe eat a donut. If you are ready to start putting the skills you have and will learn to work to build your future. Then let's get started. If you go forth let me warn you that your dreams could actually come true. The success you realize will change your life and that of your families. If you are sure you are ready for success and all that comes with it then go to the next chapter.

Chapter 2
Laying out the operational Structure

What is an operational structure of a Business? Why is it important? Is it cheaper to file bankruptcy both personally and for your business? Well let's take the first question first. An operational structure is like branches of a tree. Everything that happens on the tree does it because of the branches. The operational structure is the system that the daily operations of the business take place on. Every part of a business must be accounted for in the operational structure.

The operational structure is the basis for the road map by which you will drive your business to success. Whether it is the sales persons daily activities or how garbage is taken care of there has to be a step by step written explanation OF HOW IT SHOULD HAPPEN. You cannot know all the situations that will occur during the course of your business and your path to success. We can plan for problems that may occur and have emergency contingency plans to protect our business.

Why is it important to have an operational structure? Well we must know where we are going in order to get there. An operational structure is the road map that tells you and your employees what to do on a daily basis. If you do not have one and an emergency happens there will be problems that could ruin your business. Even if your sales grow it could ruin your business. You say that is impossible increased sales to lead to problems or failure. But what happens if you are a construction company and you grow fast and get bigger jobs. But you never planned how fast you could grow and still do a good job. You never planned how much you could grow and still cash flow the projects. Well many companies have imploded due to growing too fast with no planning.

So planning your operational structure is not only important for trouble but also for success. Operational structure is not just for the big things but for the smallest part of the business. Just like in a car's engine where every part has a function every part of a business needs to have function. If a part of a business does not have a function then it does not need to exist.

There are different structures for different industries. There is no one right structure for every type business. Every business is unique and its structure should be as unique as it. Even if two businesses are in the same industry and are the same size they are different. What is right for one may not be right for the other. To run your business based on what others do or have done is foolish. While what one business does might work for you to simply start doing it without any thought is asking for trouble. Anything that is added to your businesses operational structure must be studied and customized for your business.
It is too easy to add something to your business and say to yourself "I will decide later how it needs to fit in to the business". But when the something causes problems it is too late.

So do not skip over this section and think that is not important for to do so is to accept defeat. It is like starting to date while you are married and deciding to worry about it when your spouse finds out. It rarely ends well.

We will look at several different type industries and a basic structure for each. This is meant as a starting point. Look at the business you are about to start and use the following examples to build your structure for success. You must put the structure in writing and follow it and update it as needed. This is one of the most important things you will do in preparation for the start of your business.

Retail Structure:

We are going to look at a retail business that has one location. Our sample retail business will be a shoe store. The first step is laying out the different areas of operation. This business will have three main areas of operation.

The first area of operation will be the office. The office is the area where records will be kept and the health of the business will be controlled. The office should be able to monitor all areas of the business at any given point. Most business owners wait till their accountant gives them end of the month statements to see if they made money or need to call the bankruptcy attorney. You cannot survive driving looking backwards. You must know your numbers on a daily basis. Does it take more effort than running your business by the seat of your pants? YES! By knowing the numbers on a daily basis you might be in business at the end of the year. Once you get used to knowing what is happening in your business you will wonder why anyone does without it. How do you set up gauges in your office so that you can monitor your business?

The gauges are set up by drawing a diagram of every part of your business. Then asking what type of information do I need from this area. For example in our store we need to know how much power we use a month. We use our power bill to give us this gauge. Most are not that easy but still need to be watched. Some of the things that we need to watch are the inventory levels, orders, employee hours, employee performance, fixed expenses, variable expenses, advertising, debt service and many more. The thing to do is to set a gauge and a system to provide the gauge the information it needs. Don't be overwhelmed at this task. Simply take the list you made and start with the first on the list. Figure out how you can get information from this item for your gauge. Write down the procedure. Then move to the next on the list. When your gauges are completed then set up a reading schedule of when each gauge will be read. Some will be daily like inventory and scheduled hours. Some will be weekly like weekly sales and scheduling. Some will be monthly like power usage and a review of all gauges.

When you have this done and feel confident in how to use them. Then set up a notebook or board in the office. In this notebook or on the board you will put the gauge readings so you can follow their progress. The gauges will do no good if you do not use them. It is like buying an exercise bike to lose weight and never getting on it.

In today's age computer programs can provide much of this information at the touch of a button. It is important to your survival that you know how to gather this information and more importantly how to tell if it is off in any way. If the information the computer is using is wrong then the calculations it is making for you each morning will be wrong as well. If they are wrong it is your fault for not setting up the gauges correctly. So knowing how to do it old school is very important not just too getting accurate information but to knowing what the numbers mean.

The office must be laid out so that all the information you need is at your fingertips. The office is the cockpit of your plane. You must be able to read all the gauges without leaving the captain's chair.

The office must also be set up so that you can meet with employees and hold other meetings. You never want to discipline an employee on the sales floor. All business of the store should take place in the office. You would not eat in the bathroom would you? So don't plan your businesses future on the sales floor with all the distractions.

The second area of operation is the stock room. This is where all the inventory of the business is kept. It is important to have this area neat and everything in its place. This is not an area to put things you aren't using or to store things. This area holds your investment and the source of your income. So treat it with respect. This area should report daily to your gauges in the office. There is no need for a daily inventory because if your beginning inventory is added to shipments daily and then sales are subtracted this will give you a correct gauge of your inventory. Once a week a physical inventory should be taken to make sure everything is correct in your counts. If the count is off then you might have theft or incorrect paper work. Either way it is a problem. The sooner you know the sooner you can correct the problem. If like many businesses you waited to the end of the year to take inventory how large of a problem do you think you would have? It is also hard to find out what caused it 11 months later.

The stockroom of a retail store should also be shifted in accordance with incoming merchandise and an inventory plan should be prepared for incoming merchandise. The gauges you have in place should be checked on a regular basis to make sure you are getting accurate readings. A well planned stock room can either help your employee's make more sales by being easy to find merchandise fast or be so confusing employee's tell customers they don't have a product when you have 10 on a shelf behind someone's gym bag. When that happens it hurts not just your bank account but your blood pressure when you find out.

The third area operation is the sales floor. The sales floor is where your revenue is generated. You need to have your gauges in place so you can track not only what is being sold and for how much but how much profit is being made. The sales floor should be laid out so that your highest profit items are in a place of importance. The sales floor should be laid out for profit not just a place to stack things. The cash register and sales records should have precise gauges on them. The records should be updated daily. The information should be reviewed daily.

These are the basic areas of operations for a retail store there may need to be many more areas depending on the layout of the business. If you have an outside sales force and an inside retail floor then each would need different gauges. No matter how many areas you will have each needs a separate gauge and should be managed separately. It is vital not to take for granted any gauge. For they all are very important to your success.

Construction Structure:

The next structure we will look at is construction. This could be everything from plumbing to landscaping. The construction operational structure can be varied depending on the different type of industry. We will look at a very simple structure that can be built upon. Our construction company will have four areas.

The first will be the office. Just like before the office is where we must watch the gauges of the business. The gauges must be set up like we discussed in the retail structure. Take a look at every part of the business and attach gauges to them. The office is where all meetings will take place. Make sure that all the gauges can be read and managed from the office.

The second area of operation is bidding or sales area. This area is where jobs are won and revenue obtained. It is important to know all your costs when bidding projects. Make sure all of your costs are added in and profit is taken into consideration. Many contractors forget to take into account their overhead (Office, insurance and other expenses). They end up working themselves out of business. A system needs to be in place to put bids together and to win them.

Goals need to be set and measured on a regular basis. Your sales area should be reminded constantly of goals and expectations. Your gauges have to be constantly checked. After a job is finished see how the ending numbers compare to what they were supposed to be. If they are out of line make adjustments.

The Third area is the construction area. This is where the work is carried out. If your people don't manage their time correctly to budget then you will not make money. So putting proper gauges in place is the only way to succeed. You must know number of hours worked each day and what was accomplished. How this measured up against your plan and budget. Every piece of equipment must be accounted for and its fuel levels accounted for. In construction most theft occurs from employees doing side jobs with your tools. So gauges must be in place to watch for these variances.

The fourth area of operation is quality control. Many contractors do not think of this as a separate area of their company but it must be in order to succeed. Quality control keeps a watch out on the progress of the project and makes sure that an acceptable standard of work is being carried out. Even if you have a small company and do not have a separate department for this the gauges must be put in place. This is a separate check and balance. When you grow and add a separate person for this position it will be in place. If you do not plan for the position and gauge then you may never add it or consider the gauge. Not doing so will cost your business in reputation from mistakes and poor workmanship. This will cost revenue and profit.

As your construction company grows it is important to add different areas of operation and put separate gauges in place. If you are a service and new installation company then each would be a different operation area. It is important to know the costs of each area and the profit goals of each.

Professional Structure:

The operational structure for a professional structure can be very varied depending on its size. For our example we will use a basic structure that includes 4 areas of operation. There are many type

Professional organizations from accountants to consultants to attorneys.

The first area of operation is the business office. This is the area that controls the billing and is the life blood of the operation. Every other part of the organization must be tied to the business office. Gauges must be put in place so that at any given time the amount of payables and receivables can be assessed. In a professional setting it is too easy for work that is done never to be billed and many times work if billed is under billed. The business office must have gauges on every aspect operation. Before starting the business you must sit down and write out every function in your business. Then put a measuring gauge in place.

The second area of operation is the marketing or sales arm. This is the area that drives the client base. You must make sure that the marketing plan is following its road map for success. You must set expectations and measure them.

The third area of operation is the production area. This is every function of the operation that produces the work product. Just like with any other area goals must be set for each part of the area and they must be gauged.

The forth area is that of compliance and records. In a professional business operation many times there are special rules for record keeping. So check the specific rules with your state and make sure your business is following them. Gauges must be put in place to monitor the efficiency of the operation.

Restaurant Operational Structure:

In the restraint business like all businesses the cost must be watched or it will lead to bankruptcy court. The Restaurant business can be divided into 3 operational areas. Like we discussed before if your business is more complicated then create more areas. The important thing is to know what area each function of a business is in and be able to gauge the effectiveness of each area.

The first area we will look at is the office area. This is the area that handles the books and must watch all the other areas of the business. In setting up the office you must look at each function of the business and make sure you can put a gauge on each.

The second area of operation is the food preparation area. No matter the size of the business all restaurants will have a preparation area. Every part of this area must be held account able for the guidelines you place upon them. This is the area where food cost can either be held in check or let run rampant. Many restaurants use "Hopium" to control food cost. They hope that everything will work out so that costs will be in line. The successful business operator will set the goals and hold each area of the kitchen accountable. A system must be put in writing for the kitchen workers to follow to reach the necessary numbers. The gauges have to be in place so that the office can know daily if numbers are being met.

The third area of operation is the service area. This area comes in contact with your customers and drives your business. They are your sales force if they are friendly and up sale menu items you will be successful as long as you have gauges in place in all aspects of the business.

The service staff must know what is expected of them and how their being gauged. Some type of feedback must be used on a regular basis to gauge customer satisfaction. The gauges must be daily or weekly not when customers stop coming and you are bankrupt.

All of these areas must be watched and gauged in order to be successful. Don't wait till business crashes to start monitoring. Even if you are a sandwich shop and you say the service staff and kitchen are the same. They must be gauged differently so you can see how each area is performing.

Conclusion:

There are many more types of business structures than what I have reviewed. The main thing is to develop your own structure. List what each part of your business is doing and how you can gauge it. Then use the gauges daily in running your business. If you do not have the proper structure your business will not succeed. You must not only put the structure in place but make sure it is used by all aspects of your business. If your business grows or has any kind of change you must sit down and analyze your business. Then create new areas if needed with gauges so you can monitor the new areas.

Success will be yours if you follow your structure and watch the gauges of your business. You will not depend on "Hopium" to run your business but you know that success will be yours because of your planning and watching the gauges of your business. No longer are you at the mercy of any outside forces because you are the master of your business and the path to success.

Chapter 3
Which Type of Ownership Structure

In today's business world you need to do business with a corporate structure. There are many different types of corporate structures. What is a corporate structure and why do you need one?

A corporate structure is legally another being created to protect your personal assets from creditors and lawsuits. The entity pays taxes (with the exception of some forms that allow pass through to your personal tax return) and can enter into contracts. Entering into a new business must be done with the proper preparation and planning to insure you are protected.

You need a corporate structure because a business is a separate entity from your family and yourself so it needs to be treated as one. Setting up your business in a corporate structure enables you to gauge the health and growth of the business during its life time. In the life of your business it may on occasion be sued by entities seeking money damages. If your business loses and you have protected yourself properly even if the judgment was over your insurance limit you will be safe. Your personal assets will be protected. They are protected because the corporation that owns your business is not you personally. All of your family's assets are still yours no matter what your business does. The same holds true for loans your business may have. For a loan to belong to the corporate structure the loan must be in the name of the corporation with no co-signing by you personally. You may sign the loan documents but only as your office within the corporation. We will cover this more in depth below.

An important item many people forget to do when they do form a corporation is they do not enter into contracts or loans in the proper way. They do the right thing by forming a corporate entity but do not use it in the right way. We now will review some important things to remember in doing business as a corporation. These things cannot be done some of the time they must be done all of the time. If they are not done properly death will not be slow it could be quick not just for the business but for your personal assets.

In doing business as a corporate entity you must remember one important point. The corporate entity is not you it is a separate entity. It must be treated as one. You are simply an officer or member (Depending on the type of entity) of the corporate entity. You should sign these loans and any contract your business enters into as an officer of the corporation or the member. Nothing you do is done in your personal name it is done in the corporate name with you signing as your office. You do this by signing your name then after your name put your office. Your office would be President, Treasurer, Member and ECT. In doing this you are signing the corporation as the entity that is liable for the debt or contract. If the business cannot repay the obligation then the business is obligated to pay the debt. Not you personally.

But in order to keep the protection of the corporate entity you must keep your personal life separate from the corporate life. This sometimes called the corporate veil. If this corporate veil is broken then corporate creditors can move from collecting just the corporation's assets to collecting your assets.

To guarantee that the corporate veil is not broken you must make sure not to pay for personal things out of the corporate check book and not to pay for corporate things with your personal check book. You cannot use corporate assets for your own enjoyment without compensation. If you remember the corporation is a different entity and treats it as you would another person.

The way that compensation is taken from your business is through salary, stock dividends and officer compensation. The corporate board which you as owner pick can give perks to the leadership of the company but it must be documented. These concepts are confusing for many and many attorneys often get confused on the proper activities for a corporation. Common sense usually leads you in the right direction.

Now let's look at the different forms of corporate entities. There are others than what we will go over but these are the main forms you will use in your businesses. We will first look at the chart below that will give the names of the corporate entities and the differences in their makeup. Then we will look at each in more depth.

Different Forms of Business Entities

Entities Characteristics	LLC Limited Liability Company	C Corporation	S Corporation
Ownership Rules	Unlimited number of members allowed	Unlimited number of shareholders; no limit on stock classes	Up to 100 shareholders; only one class of stock allowed
Personal Liability of the Owners	Generally no personal liability of the members	Generally no personal liability of the shareholders	Generally no personal liability of the shareholders
Tax Treatment	The entity is not taxed (unless chosen to be taxed); profits and losses are passed through to the members	Corporation taxed on its earnings at a corporate level and shareholders are taxed on any distributed dividends	With the filing of IRS Form 2553, a C Corporation becomes a S Corporation, where the profits and losses are passed through to the shareholders
Key Documents Needed for Formation	Articles of Organization / Certificate of Formation; Operating Agreement	Articles of Incorporation; Bylaws; Organizational Board Resolutions; Stock Certificates; Stock Ledger	Articles of Incorporation; Bylaws; Organizational Board Resolutions; Stock Certificates; Stock Ledger; IRS & State S Corporation election
Management of the Business	The Operating Agreement sets forth how the business is to	Board of Directors has overall management	Board of Directors has overall management

	be managed; a Member (owner) or Manager can be designated to manage the business	responsibility; Officers have day-to-day responsibility	responsibility; Officers have day-to-day responsibility
Capital Contributions	The members typically contribute money or services to the LLC and receive an interest in profits and losses	Shareholders typically purchase stock in the corporation, either common or preferred	Shareholders typically purchase stock in the corporation, but only one class of stock is allowed

Differences between an LLC and a S Corporation

It's smart to protect personal assets from business debts and liabilities. Both owners of S Corporations and LLC's enjoy limited personal liability. By contrast, sole proprietors and partners have unlimited personal risk.

Traditionally, business owners who chose to form an entity to protect personal assets but allow income/losses to be reported on a personal tax return had to create an S Corporation. Today, that can also be accomplished with an LLC. All 50 states and District of Columbia recognize LLC's, and their popularity has soared. Nolo's Legal Guide for Starting and Running a Small Business states, "For the majority of small businesses, the relative simplicity and flexibility of the LLC make it the better choice. This is especially true if your business will hold property, such as real estate, that's likely to increase in value."

Both S Corporations and LLCs allow owners to avoid "double taxation" and to pay income taxes on a flow-through basis like sole proprietors and partners. However, LLC's are quickly becoming a preferred entity among small business. Here are some key examples of the benefits of an LLC verses an S Corporation:

1. An LLC is simpler and faster to form. It may be formed in one step
While an S Corporation election can only be made after a General Corporation is formed first.
2. An LLC is not required to hold annual meetings or to keep formal minutes, while an S Corporation is required to do so.
3. LLC members can split profits/losses in any way they choose.

In an S Corporation, shareholders must receive dividends according to the number of shares that they own, regardless of the amount of effort put into the business.
4. An LLC can be owned by any combination of individuals or business entities. Only United States citizens and resident aliens may own an S corporation .Other entities generally may not own an S Corporation.

While many business owners are enjoying the simplicity and flexibility of the LLC, it may not be the best choice in every case. If you are involved in services such as health, law or engineering you especially should consult a tax advisor on this issue. Your attorney or tax advisor will be able to explain in depth which type of entity is best for your company. If you have questions when talking to them be sure to ask them. It is the only way to get answers.

Now let's look at the individual type of entities:

Limited Liability Company (LLC)

The LLC is a type of hybrid business structure that is designed to provide the limited liability features of a corporation and the tax efficiencies and operational flexibility of a partnership. A popular choice for sole proprietors who are looking to incorporate simply to protect personal assets or secure additional loans, the LLC is thought to be one of the easiest and least expensive forms of ownership to organize. The Limited Liability Company (LLC) is now a recognized business structure in all 50 states plus the District of Columbia. LLCs are gaining popularity with small business owners because they combine the advantages of a corporation with the tax advantages and management flexibility of a partnership

What are the main advantages of forming an LLC?

1. Owners of an LLC have limited liability for business debts.
2. For tax purposes, the allocation of profit and loss of an LLC need not be proportional to ownership interests.
3. With an LLC, there is no double taxation threat since the LLC is not a separate taxable entity.
4. You do not need to be a US citizen to own or invest in an LLC.

S Corporation

A subchapter "S" Corporation, also called an S Corporation, is a corporation that once incorporated, elects a special tax status. The Subchapter S tax election enables the shareholder to pass through earnings and profits directly to their personal tax return.If the corporation has a profit, the shareholder, if working for the company, must pay themselves wages that meet the standards of "reasonable compensation."

What are the main advantages of forming an S Corporation?

An S Corporation is said to have less risk from government audits as a corporation (as opposed to sole proprietor or LLC) Owners of an S Corporation have limited personal liability for business debts. With an S Corporation, owners can use corporate losses to offset income from other states. Owners of an S Corporation can save on employment taxes by taking distributions instead of salary. With an S Corporation, there is no double taxation threat because the corporation is not a separate taxable entity.

How to Form an S Corporation

In order to form an S Corporation, proceed with the filing of a regular C Corporation since the articles of incorporation that are filed with the state are the same for both the C Corporation and the S Corporation. After you receive all the paperwork back from the state, go ahead and fill out the IRS form 2553, Election by a Small Business Corporation, and submit the form to the IRS. This S Corporation form is included in the Corporation Complete Package.

C Corporation

A C Corporation (or simply a Corporation) is considered by law to be a unique entity separate from those that own it. As an individual entity, a corporation can be taxed, sued, and can enter into contractual agreements. Corporations are owned by shareholders of the corporation, which elect a board of directors to oversee the major business decisions and policies. When ownership changes in a corporation, the corporation does not dissolve.

What are the main advantages of forming a C Corporation?

1. Corporations are said to have less risk from government audits as a corporation (as opposed to sole proprietor or LLC).
2. Owners of Corporations have limited personal liability for business debts.
3. Corporations can deduct the cost of benefits as a business expense.
4. Corporations can split corporate profit among owners and the Corporation, paying a lower overall tax rate.
5. With a Corporation, there is no limit on the number of stockholders.
6. Corporations can raise additional funds through the sale of stock.
7. You do not need to be a US Citizen to own or invest in a C Corporation.
8. You can elect <u>S Corporation</u> status if certain requirements are met, enabling the company to be taxed similarly to a partnership.

How to Find the Forms Needed To Create Your Corporate Entity

Now that we have covered the basic forms of corporations let us look at where you can find the forms necessary to create your corporation entities. If you have any questions remember you can consult an attorney. Always remember that you are in control so make sure you get what you pay for in the relationship. The first step is going to your state's web site to find the department that handles incorporations. It will be the Secretary of State's office or perhaps the state license department. It depends on how your state is set up. If you have trouble the old fashion method of calling your local county court house and ask the records room where you file incorporations. They are usually very helpful. Then call the number they give you and ask for the web site or just have them mail the forms. Every state has a little different filing procedure so, I am not going to give you a generic filing procedure because you need the exact method and they will give it to you. It is not difficult just follow the steps that are given to you.

When you file your corporate entity you will also need to get a Federal Identification number. This is obtained from the IRS. You can go to their web site or simply call them and they will take the application on the phone. It is better to go the web site print out the form and then either submit on the web or call the number given and read the information off the form.

A Federal Identification Number is a social security number for a business. You will put this on loan applications and lease applications where it says put your social. You will never put your social and the corporate name. The corporation is a separate entity and the federal Identification number is their social security numbers so don't get them confused with your personal self.

A Corporation is like a new pair of shoes. You have to break it in. It will take a while to get used to using the corporation in the proper way but eventually you will get the hang of it. Even though it might be overwhelming at first you must get the hang of using the corporate entity you set up or you and business are doomed for failure.

Don't think this is just a bunch of paper work because though it may never become an issue in your business. If it is done wrong your family and your business will not be safeguarded. So please if you will not take the time to do this step properly do not open a business buy a car with the money you were going to use for the business. Always remember when you look at the car that if you had only taken the time and opened a business the right way you could be driving a much nicer one.

Chapter 4
What to do once you are ready to start your Journey

Don't even read this if you have not went through the steps to design the proper form for your business and put in place the structure your business will need for your journey. You do have a choice now before you open your business. You can either not open the business or use your money to buy a timeshare in Orlando so you can use your abundance of "Hopeium" to dream you actually own a condo there once a year. Since you are using "Hopeium" you can even dream your best friend is Mickey Mouse. The other option is to use your road map you have prepared and drive your business to success.

Opening a business is like taking a trip on a plane. You have options either to get on the plane and let it take off or get off the plane before it takes off. Because once it takes off landing is mandatory. If you do not land once the plane takes off it means you crashed. Which is not good and more than likely will hurt. If your business does not follow the road map you have prepared then it will crash and bankruptcy court will hurt also. Not as much as crashing in a plane so remember you do have options.

So now that we have that out of the way let's take the next step on your journey. Now comes the beginning of the journey. Before you open up you must make sure a few things are taken care of prior to opening. In the next few pages I will mention a few things that will need to be taken care off and some thoughts on the item.

Charge Cards:

If you want to take in money in your business you will need to set up a charge account to take Visa, MasterCard and American Express. In order to take charge cards you will need to find a charge card processor. There are many different companies the important thing is to find out what each company will charge you and what they can do for you. In order to process charge cards you will need the equipment. They will offer to charge you a lot of money for the equipment. Make sure you negotiate a better deal on the equipment. Remember they will be making money off of you so they need to get something in return. If one company says no there are other companies. Ask if they will give you the equipment if you sign a longer contract. You have the power as my 3 year old says. So use the power to negotiate a better deal.

Watch your monthly statements once you find a processor sometimes they will slowly raise your rate or add extra fees. So always calculate what you are being charged. If they raise the rate on you remember you can you have the power so look for someone else to fill that position in your company.

Open Bank Accounts:

Your business is a separate entity and every thing must be kept separate. Your business actually needs a few accounts. When choosing a bank always find the bank that has the lowest fees on there accounts. Many banks do not even charge fees on certain type of accounts. When checking banks always delve deeper and ask questions. Like are there any accounts that have no fees and how can I reduce my fees.

In your business you will be collecting sales tax and employee payroll tax. It is to easy to spend this money and then you will rush around trying to find the money to pay the government. So it is safer to actually open accounts for your taxes. One account for the taxes will be fine but do not use this money for anything else besides to pay the taxes. You will sleep better at night knowing the tax money is in the bank. Plus if you don't pay it you could end up in jail and the TV program selection is really bad there so you want like it.

You will want a savings account for your wealth you will start to build and an operational account to pay things like rent and other bills. If you have a lot of employees it is a good idea to have a payroll account. Never use one account to pay a bill of another. Even if you say I will put the money back it is a bad idea.

You will also need an account to put your charge card money into. While you may say your operational account will be fine. When a problem occurs it is much easier to find the problem when each deposit is a day's receipt of charge cards. Also if there is a credit transaction or fee tied to charge transactions it is easier to have them all in a separate account. Once a week transfer the money to your main operations account.

Business Licenses:

You will need a business license to operate your business. You will need a state license and a local license. Many states also require county licenses. Call the number in the phone book for business licenses and find out what information you will need. They will ask you to estimate your sales for the first year. Remember your license is based on this amount so don't exaggerate this number unless you like paying more money than you have to.

Depending on the type of business you are opening you may have to have inspections done by the municipality before the license is issued. Make sure if they will be doing inspections what they will be looking for when the inspection is done.

Sales Tax Number:

This is the number that the sales taxes will be paid under with for your business. This number can be gotten from the business license office in most states. You will have one for the State, County and local government. Keep these numbers written down in your office because you will need them.

Insurance:

Your business will need to be insured and your family needs to be insured. So before you open your business you need to make sure you are covered. So you need to make a list of all of your business assets. Then get quotes from at least 3 different agents. You will need property and casualty insurance and liability coverage for your business. While accessing your insurance needs you might find that you will need life insurance on key employees and yourself. This is important because if you lost a key employee and your revenue went down the insurance would help you survive the loss.

If you are going to be in business for yourself then you must have health insurance for yourself and your family. This is a must and while you may say when the business gets going then you will get it that thought process is a mistake. Your family needs coverage and if you can not afford to get health coverage then you need to work for someone else because you will always be one hospital stay from failure.

You need to make sure you have enough life insurance to leave your family and business debt free because without you there will be a strain on the business. It is important to give your family and business breathing room in case you do die. Because even though you may no longer be on the road to success your business will still be on the journey.

Professional Services:

Before your doors are open is the time to follow the instructions for choosing your professional team members. As we will discuss in the chapter on choosing your professional team members you must hold your team members to what is expected from them. While everyone will need a different array of professionals make sure you hold them accountable.

The professionals you may need can include attorneys, accountants, contractors and marketing people. So you must look at your structure and see what professionals you need to make your business run at its optimum performance level.

Employee Selection:

Choosing your work force is one of the most important decisions you will make. The time to institute your hiring process is before your business opens. Look at your structure and see what employees business will need. You will have detailed job descriptions for each position. Because instead of hiring the people you like the best you will hire the person that best fills that position.

Make a chart stating each position and how many people you need to fill that level of positions. You will also determine when you need to hire these positions. For example if you are building out your store and need labors then hire them. You do not need sales people at that point. You should never have people you do not have a need for because if the position is gone their needs to be no person standing around wasting money till another position is found.

So once you have determined this then you must decide what is going to be the best place to find your employees. For example if you need sales people why not go to different stores and find people who do a good job. Then find out if they might want a new job. You can run ads in the paper but be prepared to get many unqualified applications. If you can pin point the best way to find people for each position then put the plan of action into place. Always keeping in mind that you are hiring your profit center or the reason you will file bankruptcy. So only hire those that you really fill will benefit your business. If you make wise decisions during the hiring process then your business will be off to a good start.

Arranging Product Shipments:

You will have already decided on your products you will carry or the tools you need to produce revenue now you must make sure that they will be there when you open. This sounds easy and it is not hard but it can cause problems if you do not plan it properly.

When you have decided when you will be ready to open and when your merchandise needs to be there then contact your vendors. You will need to arrange the shipment date and any other issues that remain. Your business cannot run at optimum performance if it has no way to produce revenue.

Marketing For Grand Opening:

Your business structure which you will have completed will include a marketing arm. You need to make sure that the marketing functions are running at full capacity when you are ready to open. Be careful not to advertise too much because those bills will come due. Advertising sales people are real nice till you can't pay their bills.

You have prepared a budget so stick to it do not exceed it and conversely do not under advertise. The best form of getting the word out is the personal touch and that is inexpensive compared to media advertising. I know you have already put the gauges in place to track all of the advertising that you do for your business. If you cannot track it then don't do it. If an advertising person comes in and wants you to buy their products. Ask them how can the results be tracked? If they cannot tell you and will not help put that gauge in then don't buy the advertising. Some examples are as follows: For coupons make sure every different advertising source has a different coupon or is marked in some way so you know where it comes from. For ads that generate phone calls or even for phone numbers on coupons or flyers make sure you use tracer numbers which statistics can be generated as to which ad the calls came from and who called. You should get a list with a phone number and person's name that called.

You must make sure that your entire marketing plan is ready not just the first month. You will be very busy and it is too easy to let the ball drop so make sure you read the gauges and make changes in the marketing plan as needed.

Utilities/Services:

I know you are thinking who would forget this but don't ever assume anything. Look at your structure and road map to determine when the different utilities need to be turned on or started. If you turn them on to soon it will cost you money. Talk to the different utilities and see if they have a program where you pay one price all the time. Most will let you pay an average so that you are not hit with a huge bill during certain seasons. When preparing your budget this is very helpful. Some of the utilities you might want to turn on are as follows: Power, gas, water, garbage, pest control, internet, laundry services and any other that your business needs. In today's emphasis on sustainable energy don't forget to check with the Federal government or your state to see if there are programs to pay for installation of sustainable energy (solar, wind and many other types). With rebates available or even some programs with free equipment this can be a real money saving program.

Arrange Temporary Workers:

In planning your road map to success using temporary workers can help run your business efficiently. Depending on your business temporary workers can be very cost effective. When you need labor or office help only for a short while then temporary workers might be the answer. The agency covers there workers comp and pays all taxes it is a great way to cover your labor needs.

The workers not only have to answer to you but to the managers at the temporary office. Don't think they will have no one for what ever your labor needs might be. They have skilled and unskilled workers it is a great resource to help control your labor costs. You only hire them for when you need them. So don't over look this important resource.

These are just a few of the things you must be aware of how to deal with when opening a business. As you can see the list is quiet long and there are many other issues we will go over in this book. So if you think it is too much for you to handle "DO NOT OPEN A BUSINESS" instead takes a trip with your money or simply just save yourself the trouble of the work it takes to open a business and simply go file Bankruptcy now. But if you feel these things are important and you will put the effort into learning about how to accomplish them before you jump out and open your business then success may lay ahead in your journey.

Your family's future depends on it! Please learn the things we talk about in this book because I want you to succeed not fail. Your family wants you to succeed but the local bankruptcy attorney is betting against you. If you follow the road map you will complete your journey and win.

Chapter 5
Hiring Professionals

Why are people nervous about going out and hiring professionals? Do you feel these people are better than you? Do they know more than you?

We all have been nervous going into an attorney's office or an accountant but we should not. They represent and perform services for us. In other words they work for us and they are responsible to us. We have the power to fire them and hold them accountable for their actions.

In the next few pages I will address different professions and some things you need to ask them and have put in the contracts and service agreements you enter into with them...

Remember when you hire an attorney or accountant or any professional service provider it is no different than hiring a salesperson or a janitor. You have the power, don't ever forget that when you are told by their office they are to busy to talk to you. That is not an acceptable answer. What would you do if your secretary or salesperson told you repeatedly that you were not important enough to talk to? Then why do we accept this behavior from our employees who happen to be lawyers, accountant, builder or consultants?

That is why it is important to read the following pages and review them before you go meet a professional to engage them for services. Because establishing boundaries in your relationship with your professional services employees is paramount to your success. They must know what is expected of them and what your expectations are for the project. The goals must be established and what will mean success and what will mean failure. The most important thing is that you must hold them accountable to what is agreed on. If you do these things the relationship will be profitable for both and not just for one. If they are not providing value to you then terminate their services. Because you are the boss and don't forget that!!!!!!!!

Now let's look at some different professions and how they should be hired and what should be expected.

Attorneys:

These can be scary people to deal with on any basis. Many attorneys act like that they don't have time for you but need your money. If you run into this type take the following actions. First take a deep breathe then look them in the eye and say you don't feel they have the skills you need for your businesses. Then get up and walk out of the office get any information you may have given them. Do not stop till you get to your car. Then drive away. This will drive them crazy and has saved you from a big mistake.

What do you need to do when looking for an attorney? Well first just like as with any project in opening your business you first decide what you need done and why. Then decide if you can possibly get the information yourself from different sources. Like the Web or your local legal library. Then if you cannot get the form or information then set up interviews with at least 3 attorneys. Before you go set up your interview questions and lists of what your expectations are for the attorney.

What do you need ask?

How do you bill? By the hour or project? This question needs to be by the project. That way you know what the cost will be. If they take one hour or twenty it does not matter.

Do they take payments? Never pay the entire fee up front. Pay small down payment say 25%. Then set up a schedule of payments at different parts of the project.

What if they make a mistake? The correction of the mistake will be done free of charge. You will be shocked how many times people pay an attorney to correct a mistake the attorney makes. They should correct on their own dime.

What is their expertise in the area you need services done? Just because they have a law degree does not mean they know anything about what you need.

How long will it take to finish work? If work takes longer do they object to a reduction in the final payment? You need to know how long the project will take and if it takes longer you should be compensated through a reduction in the fee.

How will the Attorney keep you informed of the progress of the work? You deserve to be kept informed on the status of your work. You and the attorney must agree on regularly scheduled updates. This will lessen the chances for misunderstandings during your relationship.

How long will it take for returned phone calls? Get this out of the way up front Attorneys have busy schedules and sometimes it is difficult for them to call someone back right away. They should let you know what time period to expect a return call. It might be an hour or a day. If you accept the time they give you then don't get mad they have not called you till this time has passed.

What information does the attorney need from you? Just like you should have expectations from the attorney the attorney will have expectations of you. You need to get them what they need fast and make sure it is accurate.

What type of contract or service agreement will be signed between you? There needs to be an agreement between the attorney and you. Your items need to be added to their contract (How long to call you back, if they make a mistake and ECT.).

What is their legal opinion on what you want done? This is important because you need to know if you are doing the right thing.

Who gets your file if you have to fire them? If they break your agreement and are not working like they said you will have fire them. If you have paid them as agreed up to that point you need their work product to take to another attorney. This needs to be agreed upon.

Any other questions you need to ask? Ask anything that is important to your project that you want to know.

Once you have finished the interview be upfront with the attorney and tell them you are interviewing at least two other attorney. If they ask why tell them you read a book that told you to. If the attorney gets mad then cross them off the list and go to what you were told to do at the first of this section. Any professional should understand that every client is not for them and likewise not every attorney is not for you. This is also an excellent negotiating method to get the most for your money. You take control and become the power figure in the relationship the way it should be.

Once you have interviewed at least three attorneys then review their answers to your questions. You also want to call the State Bar and see what type of complaints have been filed against them. If you find out past clients say they kept money and did not do work then cross them off the list. In making the decision you should look at the answers to the questions and which attorney you feel will work the best with you. When you have made your decision then call the attorney and bring your initial payment to them. You also need to bring them the information they needed.

During the time you have them working for you remember to hold them to the conditions you agreed to and to expect them to honor the agreement. They are your employee and if they are not performing then fire them.

If for some reason you are not happy with the attorneys work and they are not living up to your agreement. First try to work things out with them and if you cannot reach an agreement for the future of your relationship. Take the step of firing them and pay any bill you feel is fair. Then get your work that you have paid for up to that point so the next attorney does not have to start from scratch. If they will not give you your work or they are causing you some other trouble. You can contact the state bar and file a complaint. Take one last try to work it out with the attorney in good faith. Tell them you about to file a complaint then if they will not come to an agreement file a complaint. Then go on with your business with a new attorney.

Attorney's Can be valuable assets to your business but they can also drain you dry financially without any real benefit. The way you make them an asset is to set expectations and then hold them accountable. An attorney is a tool a business uses they are no magic solution and before you hire one make sure you really need one.

Accountants:

Accountants are a necessary part of any business. They provide a useful service to you and your business. But they like any professional are in business to make money so you must only use them for what you need not what they want to bill you for.

When looking for an accountant many questions need to need to be answered. Let's look at a few of the questions you must ask yourself before starting your search.

Do I want an accountant to do everything or just my year end taxes? You need to know the numbers of your business on a daily basis not just at the end of the month when an accountant does your end of the month books. Driving your business by looking at end of the month statement is like driving looking backwards-NOT TO SMART. You need to know your expenses and cash position on a daily basis. Today with the internet and computer programs there is no reason you cannot be on top of your financial data on a minute by minute basis. It is not hard with the correct record keeping.

So if you have the proper record keeping in place and you are using the data to watch the gauges of your business. Why do you need an accountant to tell you how your business was doing 30 days ago? Are you that stupid you have to have them telling you how your business is doing? If you need an accountant to tell you how you are doing and you cannot look at the data your controls are giving you. Then you do not need to open a business. You can do it!

So an accountant is needed to keep the IRS happy. So depending on the type business you might only need an accountant at the end of the year. If you use an accountant at the end of the year you need to find out what form the accountant will need your information in.

How much can you afford for accounting services? You must look at your budget and see what you can afford for accounting services. Before you start looking for an accountant you must decide how much you can afford.

Once you have answered these questions then you must prepare a list of questions to ask the accountant. Then make a least 3 appointments with accountants to interview them for the position of providing financial services for your company. Remember they will work for you not the other way around.

Just like in hiring an attorney you must remember to ask all of your questions you have prepared to help you make the decision. Don't be nervous or worried you are bothering them. You are interviewing them not the other way around. Now let's look at a few things you will want to ask your future employee.

What is their experience doing taxes for your type business? You want to know this because if they have experience working with your type business it will be easier for them to work with you. How much will they charge you to do your taxes or the work that you have decided they need to do? Find out exactly what they charge and how they expect to be paid. It is almost always to get a flat rate instead of an hourly rate. That way you know the exact cost.

What if they make a mistake are you billed to correct? Make sure you do not pay for their mistakes.

What type of information do they need from you in order to do the job you expect? You need to know the information they will need in order to complete the job. You also need to know in what form they need the information.

How long will it take to complete the work? You need to know how long you will have to wait for your information. Also if the work is late there needs to be a reduction in the fee charged.

Do they have anything against having a working agreement spelling out what their responsibilities are to you and what your responsibilities are to them? Every thing needs to be in writing. This way you and they both know what to expect from each other.

How long does it take for them to return a call from you? You need to know this because if you call them you will have a time frame to expect a call. Hold them to the time they tell you.

If they are not doing their job and you have to fire them how will it take them to give you all of your work? You need to get this out of the way, because sometimes if they do not perform you will have to terminate them and you need to know how long it will take to get your information.

Any other questions you have prepared.

Once you have ask your questions tell the accountant you will interview two other accountants and that once you have completed the process you will get back with them.
This is a great method for negotiating price and it also is only fair to be honest with them.

Once you have completed the interviews review your notes and choose your new employee. Before you inform them of your choice call the Accounting State board and see how many and what type of complaints have been lodged against them. Then call the candidate you choose and congratulate them on joining your team. Call the accountants you did not choose and tell them of your decision.

Set up an appointment with your new team member and start the relationship by putting in writing your expectations of them and what their expectations are from you. This way the boundaries have been set and the relationship can move forward.

Never forget that your accountant works for you not the other way around. So hold them to the agreement you have in place and if they do not live up to it fire them. If you have a problem when you fire them getting your work from them call and give their office one last chance to what was agreed to or you will be forced to file a complaint with the state Board. If they do not do the right things then file the complaint. Then find a new accountant using the same method and get on running your business.

Insurance Agents:

Insurance is a necessary part of business. Why do you get insurance? Why do you need insurance? These are good questions because insurance many times seems like a waste of money to most of us. But if you ever need it you are glad you had it.

There are many different forms of insurance that are covered in another chapter. In this chapter we are going to talk about how to pick the insurance agent you use for your company. You might say "Well I have an agent that does my personal car insurance, why can't I use them? Well you very well may use them but you are going into business and as we have discussed in this book every aspect of a business must be thought about and analyzed. You cannot simply do something because it is easy or simple. Because if it does not fit into that master road map we designed for the business we do not need to do it.

Most business owners simply look at price when choosing an agent but if you have the lowest price in the world but the agent is slow to respond when all hell breaks loose then it was not such a bargain. So just as hiring any other professional we want to interview and in this case get quotes for the types of insurance we will need.

Before you even call an agent you will need to decide what types of insurance you will need (Discussed in another chapter). Then what kind of coverage will you need. You will also need to decide if you want one agent for all of your insurance or separate agents. Once again you must look at your road map and see what fits best.

Then when you have decided these things then you must prepare questions that you will ask the agents when you interview them. Be prepared many agents do not understand their function and will tell you let me get you quote there is no need to ask me anything. Because they feel their only function is to win your business by being the lowest priced.

You will have to explain to them your business demands certain things from the agent that is part of your team and certain questions must be addressed so that your relationship can start off on the right foot.

What questions do you need to ask? Well what do you want to know about? Below is a list of some of the things you need to know before hiring an agent:

What is their experience handling insurance for a business in your industry? You want to know this because since you are new to the business an agent can be a valuable resource in guarding against unforesceen road blocks along your journey to success.

What can they bring to your business to make it more successful? An insurance agent should be able to tell what benefit they can be to your business. Don't take "I can get you the lowest rate" as an answer. You need service and an agent that will be there for you.

How long does it take them to return phone calls? This is important because like we discussed before if you call them you need to know how long it will take to get a returned call. If it goes over this period then you know you need to call back and ask for an immediate call.

What type coverage do they feel you need for your business? You want to get their opinion about the type of coverage you need. But remember they are sales people and everything they say should be thought about and analyzed.

If there is a problem with coverage what are the steps to correct it? You want to know if you have a problem with your insurance what they are going to do to correct it. For example they bill you too much or they cancel the policy when there is no reason to. You need to know before the problem occurs what to expect as a response to the issue. If they say that is all handled by corporate then you don't need to use them because you need someone that will help you resolve problems.

If you have a claim what are the steps to file a claim and how long will it take to get paid? This is important because this is why you have insurance. Don't assume anything. When a claim arrives and it is taking longer than expected they will say that is just the way it is. Well if it is not what they told you in the beginning then you need to call them on it.

How can I save money on my insurance? Can I get what I need at a discount by doing something or joining an organization? Ask this because you never know there might be a discount for being a member of some organization or they might know of a way to arrange the insurance so you save money. If you don't ask you will never know.

How is the payment for the insurance handled? Can it be broken up into payments? If it can does that cost anything additional? You want to know how you are expected to pay for the insurance. They would love to get it all up front but it is better to break it up into the smallest incremental payment possible.

What information do they need to quote the policy? You need to know what they need to give you a quote for your insurance.

If you both agree it will be a good idea to do business together then what will it take to bind coverage? If you decide to add them to your team then what is the process to get things rolling.

Any other questions you would like to ask?

Once you finished asking your questions give the information they need to quote your insurance. Then tell them you will be interviewing at least 2 other agents and you thank them for their time. You will make a decision once all the quotes are in and you have had time to analysis the interviews with each. When you do make a decision you will give them a call informing them of the decision.

Then when you have interview each agent and received back your quotes. Review your notes and decide on which agent you feel makes a better addition to your team. Don't take price into account until you have made your decision. If the best price is not the agent you choose then you must decide if the agent with the best price would do the job. If not then go with the agent that fits your needs best. Because in life you truly get what you pay for.

Once you have made the decision then cal the agents you did not choose and give them the news. Then call the agent you hired and get them any additional information they need to bind coverage. You and the agent must also decide when coverage needs to start. If you are 2 months away from opening then you might not need coverage till some point in the future.

Once again remember they work for you and hold them accountable. With insurance agents the insurance is a contract for coverage but you still need a short agreement that states things that both of you agreed to in your opening meeting. Like how long it will take to call you back and anything else that was agreed to in the meeting.

Once the agreement is signed and coverage has been set to start then feel confident that you have made the right decision and go on to the issue that needs to be done to make your business a success.

If you should have a problem with them and you can not resolve it. Call them one last time and give them the chance to do the right thing. Then if they will not resolve the problem file a formal complaint with the insurance commission in your state. Cancel your insurance once you have obtained coverage from another insurer. You do not want to leave your business uninsured.

Contractors:

Contractors can come in many forms from landscape to electrical. While they have many different functions they all will be part of your team. They all work for you and don't forget that.

Just like with hiring the professionals we have discussed before the first thing you must decide is what are they going to do for you and how long will they have to do it. When you have decided what they will do and gathered any neccassary documents they might need to bid the work. Then sit down and begin getting the questions you will ask prepared. Below is a list of questions you need to ask but when it is a contractor you are hiring you will need to make sure any specific questions are ask to the job at hand.

How long have they been a contractor? You do not want someone that is learning on the job.

How many jobs like this one have you done? You want to know how many similar jobs like yours they have done.

What percentages of their jobs go over the dead line for completion? This is your business and you have a road map to follow. Any unneccassary delays will cost you profit and possibly success.

Do they manage the job themselves or do they use foreman? You want to know if they are hands on or if they deligate the job. Deligation is not bad it could mean they are vedry organized but you need to know.

What difficulties do they see with your project? You want to know what they see as potential problems because we must plan to overcome problems.

If they are chosen for this project and a contract is signed what type payment structure do they work under? You want to know up front how they expect to get paid. You want a structure that pays so much at each stage of the project. Never pay for the project before they start work or pay the installment before you are satisfied with the job.

How long do they think your project will take? You want to know how long the project will take so you can make sure this contractor can fit into your overall plan.

If the contractor gets the job but does not hit the dead line do they object to a penalty? You need to know because you are going to expect to charge a penalty if they do not complete on time. Both of you need to be on the same page up front.

What type of contract does the contractor use? You want to see a copy of what they want you to sign. If you look at it and don't understand it then ask the Attorney team member to explain it to you. Never enter a contract you do not understand. NEVER!!!!!!

What kind of liability coverage and workers comp coverage does the contractor carry? He is going to be working for you and if someone gets hurt you want their insurance to cover it not yours. Their employees working on your job might get hurt you want to make sure they have coverage so you don't have to cover it.

When could they start on the project? You need to know if their time line fits yours.

Have they ever had to close a construction company they ran and did any one not get their project finished? You need to know this because contractors are famous for bidding for less than it costs and working one job to pay for another. Then when they hit the wall they file Bankruptcy. You do not want to get your job and money involved with someone who has done this.

Are they licensed where the job will take place? You want to make sure they can do the job where you are located. Do not assume they are because you could end up paying the penalty.

What do they need from you to bid the project? You want to make sure they have all the information necessary to bid the job. Don't leave anything out because it could delay project.

What if they win the project but a problem arises between the two of you. What will they do to resolve the problem? You want to know up front if there is a problem how they will handle it. If they say there want be one tell them that you hope not but proper planning will make resolving the problem much easier.

How long will it take for them to return phone calls? Once again you have to know what to expect. If they do not live up to those exectations then hold them accountable.

Any other questions you may have?

Once you have asked your questions and given the contractor the information they need to bid the project. Then tell them you will await their bid and when everything is received. Then you will review the interview notes and the bid proposals. Then you will make a decision. A sure them that you will call them either way you decided and thank for their time.

Once you have completed all the interviews and received all the proposals. Sit down and review them to see which contractor should be part of your team. Once again price is not the only consideration. You get what you pay for. Choose the contractor that overall would make the best addition to your team.

Once you have decided then call the contractors that did not get the job and inform them of your decision. Then call your choice to join your team and make an oppointment for a meeting to get the contract negotiated. Welcome them to your team.

When you start work with them and a problem occurs. Give them a chance to resolve the issue. If they will not make a final call to them telling them that you are about to call the state licensing board and file a formal complaint. If they still will not resolve the issue then call and file a complaint.

Firing a contractor can sometimes be difficult so you might need to call in your attorney team member to resolve any issues. Hopefully you will never face this but remember they work for you and time is money.

Once you have fired them hire another contractor repeating the first steps.

Any other Professionals:

If you are hiring any other service that will be done by an outside entity that is not covered above start by sitting down and making a list of what job you want this person to do for your company. Then look inside your own company structure and see if this can be done by one of your existing personal without causing any slow down of your structure. Remember that just because your company has the ability to do the job does not mean to do it yourself is the nest idea. The time it takes the part of your company to do this task must be taken into consideration. Does it take away from other needed functions in your structure? By saving a few dollars you could be costing your company thousands in missed profits.

Once you have decided whether to do it yourself or hire an outside expert then follow these steps.

Write down what the goal is for the project and what are the needed criteria to make the project a success.

How is the project going to make your company run better and more profitable?

How much should this project cost to make it financially viable for your company?

How will you fund the project?

What time table does the project need?

What skills will the person completing the project need?

What type of security (Insurance, Bonds and ect.) does the person doing the project need to protect your company?

Make a list of possible sources to find the needed person or company for the project?

Then set out to interview the prospective people?

Remember to give the criteria you have established to the person wanting the contract and let them know this is what they will be held responsible for, making happen. If they do not succeed a penalty needs to be agreed upon up front and put in the contract. Once you have interviewed everyone review the prospects and decide which makes the best choice for your company.
Then negotiate a contract for their services putting in the safe guards you decided upon.
During the project check the gauges to measure progress and if it is not in an acceptable range make adjustments.

Conclusion:

Selecting a professional to work for your company is a big step and must be done correctly. Many times we all look at hiring an attorney or other professional as a way to hand off a problem so we don't have to deal with it. This is a big problem you would never get tired of driving on a road trip and simply let the car drive itself. Just like your car professionals need direction and oversight. Your project is most important to you while professionals are skilled at their trade only you have a personal stake in the outcome. Your goal is to finish your journey and be successful so watch everything that these professionals do and say hold them accountable.

Professionals often act as though you work for them and we let them. But they work for you and if they are not performing let them know they need to change or be fired. Don't be guilty of using a form of "Hopium" on your professionals. That simply means don't hope they will do a good job but know they are doing a good job. If you follow these steps not only will you get better results and guide your business better on its journey. But the professionals you deal with will enjoy the working relationship because they will know exactly where they stand.

Chapter 6
Who Do You Need On Your Team

Do you like going it alone? Would you rather guess at what to do or get professional help? Your journey to success will be filled with obstacles and important tasks. You need a team of professionals to help your business on its journey. Every business is different and has different needs but there are many professionals that all businesses will need the services of at some point. We will go over some of the professionals and service businesses you will need to decide who to use when needed. Refer to the chapter on hiring professionals as to the process to interview and hire them.

One position you may need to fill is that of an accountant. The accountant is the record keeper of the business. The accountant will keep the records necessary to keep the IRS happy. It is up to you as to how often your business structure needs input from the accountant.

The position of an attorney is one you may need to fill. Depending on the type of business you are in will depend on how much you will use an attorney. If your business uses a lot of contracts or does business in a very litigation heavy industry you might need an attorney a lot more than if you run a retail store. But that decision is yours to make.

Some businesses may need an advertising agency. This is a firm that deals with your whole advertising budget and makes ad placements and helps design the ads. There are many small firms that will work with small businesses at an affordable rate. But this position is one you only need if you need a lot of advertising for your type business.

If you will be doing any type of construction to your new location then you will need a contractor. Read the chapter on hiring contractors carefully because this is a big decision. A right choice will make your life better a wrong choice will make it a living hell.

Most businesses from time to time need printing services. So find a printer in your area that can service your needs. Remember this is a professional so when choosing a printer follow the guidelines for hiring a professional. But since you may not have work right now simply ask general questions now and when you have a project you can get into the other areas. There are many printing companies in your area more than likely they all do the same basic work. I like ones that you get to talk to an owner not a high student that really does not care about your work. You usually can get the same prices at individually owned printers as you can at large national chains but you have to negotiate the price as with everything. A printer can be a great help in ad layouts for flyers or signs to use in your business.

At some point you will have to ship something so you need to get a shipper on your team. There are many like DHL, Fed EX, UPS, USPS and many more. If you set up an account you get much better pricing and service. Every dollar you save is money to your bottom line.

Depending on your business you will need suppliers of many products. Make a list of what you will use on a regular basis and then go out to find companies for your team.

Your business must look good for your customers so if you do not have people in your structure that can do the cleaning this is a professional you will need on your team. When you are looking for a cleaning company do not forget that the cheapest may not be the best fit. You must remember to take into account whether their workers are bonded and insured. You must decide if you need this professional on your team because you will have employees that can service this need as long as it does not interfere with their other jobs.

You may also need an employment service for temporary workers. As we will talk about later in the book this is a great resource for extra labor when needed. Find an agency that can meet your needs. When you need things moved or put up they are a much more economical way to move heavy objects or move stock than hiring say a moving company. They usually have a 4 hour minimum and are great workers because they must answer to the temp service if they do not do a good job. They are insured so you do not have to worry if something is broken or someone gets hurt. But you must make sure they are insured and clearly lay out what is expected from them.

Another part of your team is the local police department, fire department and other city service providers. They perform an important and vital role to all of us in our society. We all take them for granted until something happens. When you are preparing to open try to meet the policeperson that patrols your area. Introduce yourself and thank them for the job they do. This makes them feel good and helps you know who they are if a problem occurs. For the fire department maybe stop by the fire house in your area and say hello. Remember they are also potential customers and advertisers for you.

If you are not a computer expert you may also need a computer service to work on your systems. It is better to have one chosen before a problem occurs than to wait till you need it to run payroll in three hours and have to start calling. So find someone close and who meets your needs.

You company will also more than likely need an internet provider for your company. Just like anything else you must decide what you needs are before you start looking. Then get quotes from several providers.

Your business will also need telephone service. So choose a provider for your team. You may find that a company that offers phone and internet may be your best option. Most phone, cable and DSL companies offer these services in bundle packages.

Your company will need an insurance agent. Please refer to the chapter on how to hire a professional for information on what steps to go through when hiring an insurance agent. This is an important position for your company. Do not simply take your accountants, attorneys, pool cleaners or anyone else's recommendation without first following the guidelines laid out in the chapter on hiring professionals. Your business has different needs than anyone who recommends someone to you. If you were dating and someone said you really need to marry this person or that person you would want to check them out first to see if they met your needs. I maybe should not say that because with the divorce rate what it is maybe that is how people are choosing their mates.

Conclusion:
Depending on your type business you will need different members on your team. The important thing is to remember that they all work for you. You have the power don't forget that. They depend on you for work to feed their families. The same fears of failure you may have they have so don't be intimidated by them. We all have a tendency to be awed by certain professions like Attorney's, Doctor's, Accountant's and any other profession we do not fully understand. The great equalizer is knowledge or knowing where to get the knowledge. Because knowledge is power and they no matter how grand are simply your sources of knowledge.

So choose your team wisely and never forget they are your team. These services will help you on your journey to success or through up road blocks it is your decisions which they will be.

Chapter 7
Planning Your Employee Structure

How do you hire employees? Is your cousin available to work? Your employees are the part of your business that can make you or break you. They are who the customer sees and the ones who fill their car with your inventory.

So how do you choose an employee? Well first you do not hire employees you fill positions. The difference is that instead of hiring your best friend you hire someone that has the skills you need. Only look at the skills the person has and how they can benefit your business. Your business needs certain skills in certain positions you must always remember that the skills are what you are looking for not just a person.

Before you ever start to run an employment ad you must look at your operational structure and write down every position you need. Then write down every skill that a person would need to do that position. You also need to look at what do you expect from each position. What do you need from this position to make your business make profit?

You must take each position and skill set put them on paper. With this you will begin to build job descriptions for ever position. When you interview a potential employee you will use this to make sure you stay on track and only hire people with that skill set. You will also make sure that anyone you hire knows what is expected from them.

Once you hire someone you must have gauges in place so you can monitor their efforts. You must set up a schedule when you before you hire them to regularly review their performance. During this review you must make sure they are on track and fulfilling what your business needs from them. You need to ask them to do a self evaluation on themselves. This will include listing what they are doing that they could improve on and what they can do to improve. They should also list what they think can be done to improve their position and the company. Then they should list what they do well.

This list should be give to you before your review with them so you have time to go over it.

You should prepare your own list independently of the employees list and then compare the two. When you have the meeting let the employee start with their list first and listen to what they say. Be supportive and lead their conversation in the direction you need them to improve in. Then when they are through go over anything they might have missed. Thank them for their efforts and the time they put into their review. Your employee and you work up a set of goals for them to accomplish before the next review. It is important not to set goals but list how they are going to accomplish the goals. Use these reviews as a way to fuel your businesses growth.

If during the course of your business there comes a time that a employee does not
Meet the goals you need for your business and you have to cut ties with them. Make sure before you open your business you check and see what your state's laws are in regards to firing an employee. You need to know how to terminate an employee legally but terminating an employee should always be a last resort. It costs too much to train a new employee. The goal should always be to correct the employee's actions and make sure they are not performing to standards because you have not given them the tools they need.

Once you have hired the staff you need you must make sure you have control of the direction of your business. You must have the gauges in place to monitor the actions and productivity of all your employees. It is to easy just to get caught up in day to day running of a business and for get to keep your staff heading in the right direction.
But if you are to stay on the right course during the journey to success you must know the condition of your employees on a daily basis.

What are you going to pay your employees? You must have some type of incentive program for all employees. No matter the position an employee fills you must have an incentive program to reward performance. If an employee accomplishes all the goals that you laid out for them then they deserve a bonus. Because if you did your job and set each position in your business where if they hit their performance goals you will make a profit then they deserve a bonus.

Incentives help keep your employees motivated to do better than their best plus it helps your business stay on the route the road map calls for. Employees can either be your most important asset or your worst nightmare it is really up to you.

Remember employees are people too! So even though it is hard sometimes to not have tunnel vision when the problems of the day hit you and your business you must remember to always treat your employees with respect and appreciation. They work hard for you and your business. So when they do a good job encourage them and let them know on a daily basis. If you do the rewards will be great.

Your employees are an important asset if you do your selection well. So just like any valuable asset they must be protected. You need to have insurance available for them to purchase if they wish. Many people have health conditions that make it impossible for them to get individual policies for their families and themselves. Health insurance is expensive so you will not be able to pay the total premium or possibly any of it. Just getting a group policy set up is important to your employees and their families.

You can do this by simply contacting an insurance agent and tell them what you want. Remember to get three quotes and look at what the policies offer don't just take the cheapest. The employees that wish to purchase it can and you need it for yourself as well. Everyone needs health insurance so do not open your business without planning a way for them to get insurance.

So take forming your employee job descriptions seriously and do not hire people but fill positions. Fill them with people with the needed skills and make sure they know what is expected of them. Gauge your employees on a daily basis so you can see if any part of your business needs to be corrected so you can maximize profits. If you do this your journey will lead you to success and a feeling of fulfillment like you never imagined.

Chapter 8
Finding Your Capital Too Start Your Business

Where are you going to find the money to start your business? How much do you need? Will I borrow my way to Bankruptcy? Can I get a loan? Do I want a Loan?

One part of your road map you have prepared should be an estimate of what you need to open your business. This will include equipment, inventory, advertising money, operating capital, needed insurance, businesses license, facility expense and any other item you need for your business. All of these things must be obtained in order to start your business. As we have discussed through this book there are ways to obtain items needed to start your business besides buying them and spending your capital. You will need money to start your business. Under no circumstance should you open a business if you do not have the money or items to keep your business alive. If you do you are only setting your course straight for the Bankruptcy court.

Nothing is worse than starting a business and starting the journey to success and getting close to success. Then have your money run out and the business fail in sight of success.
If you prepare a good road map and follow it to success your business will be successful.

There are many different places to find the things you need to get your business going. Below you will find a list of some of the places you can find the needed items.

The Landlord: As the chapter on finding your location will mention the landlord will often provide build out money that can be used to open your business.

Banks: Your local bank can be a source to find funding for your business. Banks only lend if you don't need the money they are not very helpful to small business owners.

Venture Capitalist: A fund raising technique for companies who are willing to exchange equity in the company in return for money to grow or expand the business. Venture capital firms often want a high rate of return (20 %+) and will finance the business with $500,000 to millions. If you choose this form of funding you must be careful not to be taken advantage of or ripped off.

Angel Investor: An individual who provides capital one or more startup companies. The individual is usually affluent or has a personal stake in the success of the venture. Such investments are characterized by high levels of risk and a potentially large return on investment. This is another form of funding that you must be careful when seeking.

From Vendors: The companies that you are purchasing can help fund your opening. Remember unless you ask you will not know. Your vendors can help pay for displays for their products. They can also put merchandise into your business and let you pay for the merchandise as you sell it. This is called floor planning and many companies have plans that will allow this.
Savings: This is the best place to fund your business. Debt can put your business on the path to failure. If you fund your business using vendors, the landlord and your savings then you will have no heavy debt load that can break the back of your business.

Many people think that all they need to be successful is sales and borrowed money. In order for a business to survive it needs to have as little debt as possible. If at all possible knowledge must be used to replace borrowed money.

Being creative and using knowledge to obtain what you need is the best way to fund your business. If you must borrow only the minimum needed and make sure your road map pays it off as quickly as possible.

So make your list of items you need to start your business and then take each item individually. Then with each item figure out how you can obtain it. First look at all the options to obtain the item without money. Then if you must purchase it find the way to obtain the item for the lowest cost. Every dime you save puts you one step closer to success.

The journey to success will be difficult with many road bumps but if you follow your road map to success your journey will end at success. So make sure every action you take in funding your business is thought out and that it works with the road map. If it does not go with your road map then do not do it because all it takes is one blow out on your journey and the journey could end in failure. You never know which action will cause the blow out so use the steps that have been outlined in the book to make decisions to improve your chances for a blow out free journey.

Chapter 9
Finding Your Location

Where do you want your business located? How much do you want to pay for rent? Do you want to own your building? What is overhead? What are CAM charges? What is overage? These are all important questions that need to be answered before you begin your quest on the road to success.

Picking the right location is a vital step in putting your business on the road. In picking the right location many factors need to be looked at and measured to see which one is the correct choice. Everyone wants the best location with the most traffic. But you must make sure you can afford the location and if you were to rent the location would your operating structure be able to pay for it.

In real estate they classify locations as A, B and C locations. The A locations are the best these are right on the main traffic patterns. The B locations are the ones just off the main traffic patterns. The C locations are the ones customers have to be looking for you to find your location.

Which one is best? Which one can you afford? Well it depends on your needs and your road map for success. If you are in a retail business then the closer you are to an A location the more traffic you will have. But if you are a contractor then a C location might be fine because you just need an office and a place for your equipment. So you first have to decide what type of traffic I need for my business. Then you have to decide if you choose a less desirable location how will you drive customers to your location. Some retailers always choose a B location because they use the savings in rent to advertise and drive business to their location. Even if you are in an A location you still must have a marketing plan because even if customers drive by your location they must have a reason to come in.

No matter which location you choose the most important thing is to make sure the location fits your road map. Just like every other part of your business your location must work well with your other areas of the business. Once you have chosen the location where you would like your business then you must negotiate the lease for the property.

The first thing you must do is decide how much you can pay for the location and still have it fit your road map. Once you have that number figured out then write it down and no matter what do not pay more than your road map will allow. It is easy to get caught up in wanting the property and pay way too much per month. Then in Bankruptcy court you can tell the judge what a nice location you had and how you might have paid too much.

In negotiating remember the landlord wants to rent to you more than you want to rent from them. Don't jump at the first offer see what the landlord can do for you and your business.

If you need capital to build out your location or help buy inventory it is possible to get money from your landlord. Often the landlord will give you build out money but this money can be used for anything. So if you do not actually need to use all the money for building out your location then use it to invest in your company. Usually large landlords will do this for you. Small landlords do not have the capital to do this most of the time. Also remember if they offer $20,000 for build out money never take the first offer ask for more. The money for the build out in reality is added in to what you are paying in rent so if you do not need the money ask for lower rent.

Another thing you must remember when looking for a location is that if you can find another business that is set up the way you need your business set up then that might be a good place to rent. If someone else has spent the money let's say to build out a sub shop and that is what you want to open you can save a lot of money by renting their old location. If the location is bad or there is some other problem then it might not be a good location. Many times though the location is great the previous owners just did not know what they were doing. They had no road map just an appointment in Bankruptcy Court.

Remember when deciding on a location you must find out the CAM (Common Area Maintenance) charges. This is not part of the rent but can be a very expensive. You must figure this cost in with your rent. Many people think they have their budget in the right amount because instead of using a road map that ties every part of the business into the others. If they had a road map they would realize that the CAM (Which is the taxes, insurance for the development, maintenance, advertising for the development and other items that are tied to the development the location is at) was going to make their numbers out of focus. So you must keep the CAM amount in mind when negotiating the rent. Also try to get the landlord to put some type of cap on the CAM. Landlords do not like to do this but they will if ask. Many numbers that go into CAM can be kept down if the landlord operates the property in the right way but why should they do that if there is no cap on what they can charge you.

When you are negotiating the lease ask the landlord to contribute to grand opening advertising. It does not have to be money remember we talked about finding out what different people can do for you and your business. So ask what they can do to help your business be successful by having a great grand opening? They often are running

Advertising for the property as a whole if you are in a mall is something you will end up being forced to do. The CAM charges pay for this expense. They could mention your grand opening in their advertising or if they have a reader board coming into the property they could list your property as having a grand opening. If they cannot accommodate you ask for money to advertise because when you are successful it helps them.

When your lease is negotiated make sure that the lease is in your corporate name not your personal name. The lease is for your business not your personal self. If they want a personal guarantee then only give a limited guarantee. Give one for a year or two not a long one but I would not give one at all. But that decision is yours if they want your business as a tenant then they will lease to your corporate entity.
There are so many topics that could be discussed in regards to negotiating leases and choosing a location that it really could another book. What I do in this book is to give you the broad strokes on what to look for and things you may not be aware of in

regards to the topics I discuss. You are not expected to be a real estate negotiating expert. But you must keep in mind what your business needs and make sure the lease does that. You will have other members of your team that understand the legal part of the equation so let them do their job but keep a eye on your gauges during negotiating to make sure everything is on track. When the lease is done and your attorney says sign make sure you read it carefully at home or your office (But by yourself). If anything does not sound right ask what it means and why it is worded that way. If they can't answer the question to your liking do not sign because you are the boss.

The decision of where your business will make its home is an important one that needs to be made with thought and analysis. Don't let emotions get involved it needs to make sense on paper and it needs to be in line with your road map. If you keep these things in mind as you are looking for a location and negotiating the lease then you will be successful.

Chapter 10
Financial Gauges for Your Business

How will you know when you are making a profit? How will you know when you have to much extra money? When will checks start bouncing? When will supplies start not shipping? What time is your appointment with the Bankruptcy judge?

The answer to all of these questions is the same. You will know when you have your financial numbers for your business. If you only look at your numbers when your accountant gives you month end numbers then the later questions will apply to you. But if you have the correct gauges in place so that on a daily basis you know your expenses, sales and where you stand compared to your plan you will be asking the first few questions. You must know where your business stands whether the numbers are good or bad. In order to drive your business to success and make corrections on the road to success you must know the real numbers.

From these numbers you will know how to guide your business over the next day and week. If you are in a retail business and the road in front of your store suddenly is under construction which makes it hard for customers to get to your store. If you know your numbers then you can adjust your employees work schedule and cut back on shipments. You do this because you know that at the end of the week you will have little money and your employees will want to be paid. With these adjustments you reduced your payroll and cut back your accounts payable so the financial strain was not a life ending event. It was simply turned into part of the road that you are traveling to success.

If you do not know your numbers on a daily basis and do not plan strategically then the road construction will surprise you. You will think maybe I ought to do something but I don't know where I stand or what actions to take. Then you will think well hopefully my business will survive to the end of the month so I can see how this affects the business. But by the end of the month you have missed payroll and your employees are upset. The suppliers are getting worried because you are late. You think the construction was only for a week how bad could it be. But you usually did $10,000 a week on average and the week in question only brought in $2,000. Where is the other $8,000 going to come from? Since you did not cut expenses to lessen the blow this money will have to be found somewhere else. Like your personal bank account or your families assets. This is a prime example of living on "Hopeium". If you had just read your gauges of course you first have to have them in place. So remember while sometimes stupidity is bliss it will cease to be blissful when you are homeless.

Now that we have looked at why it is important to have financial gauges in place I hope you will not skip to the next chapter. I call the gauges financial instead of accounting for a reason. When we say accounting it is natural to think of accountants but the accountant does not care if you are homeless unless you owe them money. So you have to know your financial numbers on a daily basis your accountant gives you a look out the rear view window. You cannot drive your business looking out the back window constantly. Knowing where you have been is important to readjust your gauges for the journey. You must also know what you are about to hit in the road. Just like an engine in a car needs every part to run effectively. A business needs all of its areas to be connected and running in a common direction.

How do you put these gauges in place? Well first you must look at your operational structure and look at every area on the outline. Then figure out how each of those areas can be gauged for a financial reading. No matter whether it is the sales area, manufacturing areas, human resources areas, inventory control areas and any other area of your business because financial numbers are more than sales they are every part of your business and the revenue produced or money burned. You must know what these numbers are and more importantly how they affect your business.

Remember when creating the gauges of your business that you cannot be everywhere at once. So create forms and gauges that your employees create and give you the numbers on a daily basis. You will check up on the numbers on a regular basis to make sure they are being gauged correctly. The gauges must be read every day and week. These numbers will be used to forecast and drive the business.

Just like driving a car and watching the gauges you only are concerned with a gauge when something is wrong. So even though you will be watching many gauges every day you will only jump on the gauges that need to be corrected. By correcting your gauges on a daily basis you will keep your business on the right path on the journey to success.

The accountant you hire can help craft these gauges so that the numbers you are reading are real. But you need to know current numbers remember so the information your accountant prepares at the end of the month or quarter is not enough. But they can help you get daily numbers if you tell them what you want.

While getting your financial gauges in order is not exciting it can keep you on the road to success and once you have mastered it you will feel better than ever. Like I have said before you must know where you are going in order to get there and the financial gauges you set up will give you this needed information.

Chapter 11
How to Know When You Are Making a Profit

Do you know when you are making a profit? Do you know at what point you reach your break even? How many widgets must you sell to cover your rent and payroll? When is Bon Jovi coming in Concert? How do you pay for tickets to the Zoo if you don't know when you're making a profit? Do you really care about any of this? Can you answer any of these questions?

Now it is extremely important that you know at what point your business goes from paying creditors to paying you. Why do you need to know this information? If you know this information then you can be more competitive when marketing and planning your sales strategy.

In order to explain this concept I am going to use an illustration of a water funnel. The top funnel is made up of all your variable expense. These are the expenses that you only incur if you sell or make a product. Expenses are like the cost of goods or the cost of the packaging for the product. The labor that goes into making your products or selling your products is a variable expense. Any expense that you do not incur if you do not sell or make a product is a variable expense.

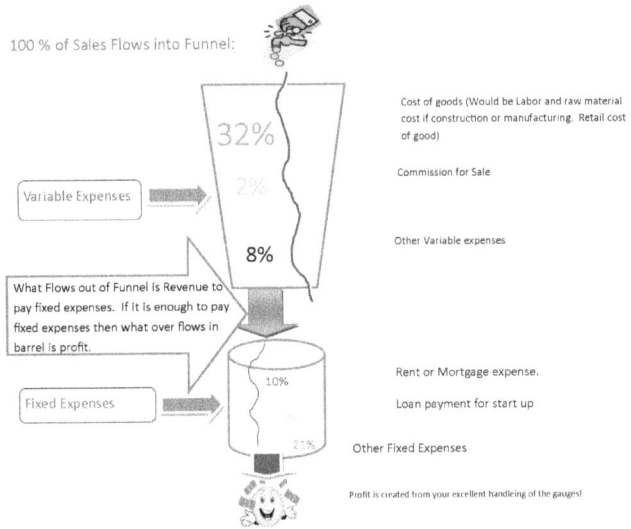

At the bottom of the funnel is a water basin that when a drop of water (A sale) falls through the funnel (Variable costs) what comes out is the difference between 100% of the sale proceeds and the variable costs (in our example it is 42%). The difference falls into the water basin. The water basin represents the fixed costs of the business. These expenses do not change. You have to pay them even if you do not make a sale. They do not go up or down. Now as you make sales the water (Sales) falls through the funnel (Variable expenses) the difference falls through into the water basin. The water builds and starts to fill the basin as you continue to make sales. When the water basin fills up at some point during the month it starts to overflow. What over flows is profit at this point every dollar over your fixed cost is profit for your business.

If you think of this simple illustration you will be able to know at what point during the month you start making money. This information will give you a competitive advantage in running your business. So now get a sheet of paper and draw the funnel. List all of your variable expenses and the draw the water basin. List all of your fixed expenses. Make copies of the diagram. When you open your business keep track of these numbers it will make you a better driver for your business. Your employees need to know these numbers because part of their responsibility is to keep expenses below you budgeted percentages. When your business works as a team it will make it to your goal at the end of your journey success.

If you need to run a sale to move merchandise and you know your fixed expenses have been covered then you can sell select items for less to increase traffic. You know that every dollar over the variable expenses is profit. Remember this starts all over again at the first of the month.

If you are a contractor and you are bidding on a job then you can bid lower if you know your expenses have been covered. If you start to think of this diagram when making business decisions you will succeed. When things are wrong in your profit model you simply adjust your funnels and prices so that success will be yours.

Many people feel they do not have time to do numbers that is what accountants are for but you are in charge of making a profit not the accountant. You can use the accountant's knowledge to help you make decisions but the decisions are yours. Accountants look behind you business to the past. They use numbers that have been already produced. You must be able to create the number you need by planning for the future. If this is done correctly you will already know the numbers the accountant came up with because you planned it that way.

If you use these easy techniques it will help you mentally grasp the idea of profit and you will find that like a ninja master that feels their very environment you will know what your business is doing because you will feel the numbers you planned and put on the road map to success.

Chapter 12
How to make a Business Decision:

In business we make decisions on a daily basis. Those decisions will also put you out of business. So for any of us to be successful we must track our decisions and have a method as to how we make the decision. You may say I make decisions quick that are fine but can you express why you made the decision years later. It is important to learn from everything you do and in order to do that you must be able to track the process. Below is a process to make decisions. Will you use it to decide where to eat- hopefully not but you should use it on any decision that will affect your business for more than a day.

First define what you are actually deciding. Meaning answer the following questions:

What is the purpose of this decision (growth, Profit, Saving Money, Expanding staff because of work load and act.)

What is the goal of this decision (similar to purpose but refine answer down to one sentence)? This should be the goal statement for this decision.

Have you made a similar decision before? (Has there been something similar you have done in the past)

What was that decision and how did it turn out? (Was decision good or bad)

Why was it good or bad for the company?

Now that you have defined for the company what you are deciding and you have developed a statement of purpose. You can look first at the decisions you have made in the past. Did you make good or bad decisions in this area? If they were good look at what was good about them and make sure you follow the example. If they were bad then put in a written form why the decision was bad. Make sure you write down what you did wrong and things to watch out for concerning this decision.

Take a piece of paper and write at the top your purpose statement. Then start to answer the following questions.

How might the company achieve its goals? (What are the options you have available to you)

Then get new sheets of paper and write at the top of each the options you have in achieving this goal. Then answer the following questions on each goal.

What would need to be done to pursue this option? (What actions need to be taken)

What would the cost be to pursue this option financially and in person hours? (What are the real costs associated to pursuing this action)

What would the biggest obstacles to success be to achieve this obstacle?

What would be the benefits from pursuing this option? (What are the advantages of this option)

Now review each of your options taking into account all the questions. Choose the option you like best, the one that cost the least and the one that benefits the company the most. If it is the same one then your decision is almost over but if not then Look at the options left and take another sheet of paper and list the three options. Then answer the following questions:

How would my employees act toward each option? (Would they like it or react negatively toward it)

What are the tax advantages to it?

Can it be financed or paid for easily?

What will the useful life of the option be?

Does this option have other benefits other than the one at hand? (Does it help in other areas also beside the statement of purpose)

Will it make management's daily job better?

Will it allow me more time with my family?

After listing these questions then analyze each option. Choose the option that makes the most sense. Then refer back to your statement of purpose and see if this option meets that need. If it does then choose this option and pursue it. Not all of these questions may be pertinent but through time you will learn to ask questions. That is what this exercise is all about. It is making you make decisions rationally and not from emotions.

It is easy to just decide something in a business but it takes time to correct it if it does not kill you business. So it is better to take time and make decisions based on facts not emotion. Save these papers on each decision so you put them in a book. Call it your book of decisions. When you see that the decision is right or wrong then go back and add a page that details what was right about the decision and anything you might change in the decision making process. If it was wrong then write how it was wrong and where the process went wrong. This will allow you to truly see where you went wrong and learn from not only the mistake but how you came to the decision.

Are you reading this thinking "This is a bunch of crap!, because no one takes this much time to make a decision!" well you are not alone. If you choose not to do this then when you file bankruptcy after your business fails ask those people who are seeing the bankruptcy judge how they make decisions. You will hear that they too did not take time to analysis their decisions so you will be proven right most people do not do this in making decisions. If you want to be successful you will and once you start having success you will actually like it.

You might even be thinking that if you do use this process to make decisions you are not going to keep a notebook of past decisions and there is no way you are going to review them. You might be thinking that remembering your mistakes and bad decisions is the job of your spouse. You figure they are doing a good job at not letting you forget every bad decision you have ever made but would it not be nice to correct future bad decisions so all they would have to say is how great you are (Unfortunately they will not do this but would it not be nice).

Remembering your past mistakes and your past victories is very important. There is a saying that "We must always remember the past least we repeat our mistakes". This is very true not only for Countries but for individuals also. It is individual decisions that make Countries and businesses go toward a path of failure. So reviewing your past mistakes and victories will make us better decision makers. By doing this a form of self analysis will be taking place. And you will find the answers to questions of why things happened in the past. By doing this you will see where your decision making process has went off track in the past. You will enter a place in your life where you will not hope a decision is right but know that is right.

That hopefully you found that humorous enough that you will remember to follow these steps in making decisions. One major problem we all have in doing reviews of decisions is that we are fine with reviewing when things go right but we don't like looking at bad decisions. Through analysis of why you made these decisions and seeing if at some point do you drop the ball is the only way to improve. It will be tough but you must look at the process by which the decision was made. When you do answer the following questions:

What was the outcome of the decision?

How did it differ from the desired result?

Why did the decision go bad? (Was it external forces or was it a problem in your reasoning)

What could have been done in the decision making process to make it correct?

What actions can be taken now to turn this decision around?

What lessons have you learned from this experience?

By asking these questions it will help you discover the reason you made the decision. It might turn out you made the best decision possible with the information you had at the present time. Not all decisions that turn out wrong are bad decisions. Sometimes things happen outside of your control but this is rare. By having the proper road map even when decisions go bad you can be ready to make adjustments that makes the bad outcome of a decision simply a bump in the road.

If you still decide to keep making decisions and never looking back. I would like to give the people reading this book that think these are good ideas but I don't need help I can fail on my own a little bit of advice. Which is when you are going before the judge at bankruptcy Court don't wear the Rolex your uncle bought you for graduation because the family thought you would be successful or carry the Coach bad because the Court may decide to take these items to help repay your creditors who also believed in you at one time.

There is no guarantee that every decision will be right that is the reason life is enjoyable. But through proper planning we all can cut down on decisions that go wrong because of not enough thought.

Chapter 13
How to Run Your Gauges

Now you have all of your structure created and you have gauges in place to monitor all the different areas of the business. It is important to use them in correct way. It does no good to have your gauges give readings if you do not use the information.

You must use the readings from the gauges to help plan the direction of your business. Not only to set goals but to monitor your progress during the journey. It is important to set aside a specific time to actually have a meeting and spend time looking at the real numbers to set and analyze the gauges.

Before the beginning of the year or before the business opens you need to set your goals for the year. You first must know what your profit percentage on each of your products and all of your expenses this information is needed to set your goals for the year.

The next step is figure out how much money you want to make for the year. This must be a real number that can be accomplished. Then once you have figured out what you want to make then you look at your sales mix and figure out what your business needs to sell in order to make your desired profit.

By doing this you do not let "Hopeium" run your business but you have put the beginnings of a plan together to reach your goals. When figuring out the needed revenue to reach your goals you need to know your expenses. You take all of your expenses and add them up take this number and add it to your profit goal. This should give you the needed revenue number to make your desired profit.

Use these numbers to set your daily, weekly, monthly and yearly goals. You not only set revenue goals but expense goals. All of these goals must be gauged and monitored. The expenses are what kill your profits so you must keep them under control.

Now at your goal setting session for the year you need to put all of these numbers down on paper. Once you have what mix of products you need to sell to reach your numbers. Then start putting together your marketing plan to reach the revenue goals. Then take the structure that you have built and assign the responsibility for reaching the revenue goals to the different areas of your business. Even the areas that are non revenue producing have responsibilities. Their responsibilities are to control expenses which are just as important as producing revenue.

You must assign the responsibilities in a realistic manner. If the numbers are not real there is no reason to do this work. Because if the numbers are not real then every reading you get will be wrong. Once you have a chart built of what each department must do to reach the goals and what numbers they must meet then review it and finalize it for the upcoming year.

You then can have meetings with all of your staff and review what the numbers are and how they will reach them. You must extend the responsibility down to every person in your company. Because everyone that works for you will either help or hurt your businesses performance. It is up to how you handle it as to which outcome it will be. The struggle will be what they must accomplish and monitoring their progress and helping them achieve the goals.

Before you achieve your goals you must know what they are and what would be success. So the following form is to help you define your goals. In doing all these sheets remember to be honest this is important to your future. Do not set goals that are to lofty. Set real goals that you can reach because this is the beginning of your journey harder goals will come like a journey of a thousand miles it begins with the first step. This is your first step so make sure it is done properly because all the steps that are to follow are based on this first step.

If there are things you don't like then edit it but keep the purpose and end result the same. Because is not suppose to be a fantasy sheet but real goals that can be achieved. If you are married your spouse needs to be part of this process it will not only bring you closer together but help to make sure both of you are on the same page.

There is a signature line at the bottom this is for all business owners and their spouses because if you have not figured it out yet your spouse is a big part of your life. Even if they say it is your business and they don't want anything to do with it they really do. That very statement is telling you they might not think proper planning went into your business.

Direction and Goals for Business and Life

The purpose of this is to make sure everyone is on the same page when deciding goals for the business and life. You cannot simply say I guess this is what we want but you must know for sure. If everyone is not in agreement then problems occur.

So think about what you want from the business and from your life. Then write a purpose statement that will define everything you do. After that decide what business you want to be in and why. Then list the major obstacles you will face in this journey and the plan you will put in place to overcome these issues. Success will be yours if you plan and execute well.

The journey may be difficult but with a defined purpose and a common goal the journey will end at success. Your journey will be much happier and successful when everyone is on the same page.

So start out with you purpose statement and go from there with success being your destination. The route you take though must be planned out and followed.

Purpose Statement:

What Business do we want to be in:
Goals for this business:

Major Obstacles to the company achieving Goals:

We agree to this purpose statement and to these goals. We will work hard not to let these listed obstacles or any other problems stop us on our journey to success.

Yearly Meetings Form

New Year Planning Meeting

This is the time to stop thinking of the current year and begin the process of starting the next year. This meeting is done after you have had time to reflect on the end of the year meeting and get those issues under control. This meeting should be completely focused on the upcoming year and forming the goals of the year.

This is an important process because it will shape your direction for the entire year. If done properly it will set your journey toward success off on the right road. The year will be spent in a mode of success instead of one trying to correct problems. So take a deep breathe and start the process of planning your new year.

Like other forms you might have specific needs that need to be addressed so make additions to this form if needed. It is you business and your form so make it yours.
Start thinking of the New Year and where you want to be at the end of it.

The Purpose statement:

At the beginning of each year a statement defining your goals for the year should be worked up and it should be one that is referred to the rest of the year.

What is the statement of purpose for this year:

What are the 5 major road blocks that lay ahead on the journey to profitability this year?

How can these obstacles be overcome?

What are the sales goals for the New Year? (Should breakdown every revenue generating part of the business)

What are the goals monthly? (All business have busy times of the year and slow therefore the yearly goal needs to be allocated monthly according to your industries business cycle. If you do not know this please do not open this business)

January _____
February _____
March _____
April _____
May _____
June _____
July _____
August _____
September _____
October _____
November _____
December _____
Total of Months (This should equal yearly goal)
_____

What is the marketing plan to reach each of the
Set goals? (Look at each area of sales and define the marketing plan that will guide in reaching that goal) _____

What are the goals for controlling expenses?
_____

What steps need to be taken to help these goals become reality?
_____

Are any employee modifications needed to aid reaching the goals? (Do you need to add staff or change staff)

When are these changes going to be implemented?
_____

Are we dedicated to success of this business?
_____

What changes in inventory or products need to be done to help reach these goals? __

How can these changes be put in place?
_____

What other items need to be completed to ensure success for the year?

Do we fill this is the best program we can put in place for the up coming year? _____

By signing below we certify this New Year set of goals and plans has been discussed and improved. We feel confident we will be successful and can manage our business with these goals and the statement of purpose can be fulfilled.

Quarterly Meetings

Your goals and progress must be monitored every so often to make sure you are on track. By every so often I mean all the time. When you start going off course it is easier to correct the course a mile of the right course than when you are completely lost. So below is a form to be used once a quarter. It is to be filled out and saved for review.

The Purpose of this meeting is to look ahead on your journey to success at the end of the year. During this meeting the ownership needs to address the past quarters and see how the business is verses the plans for the year. Then you look at changes that need to be made in your plan to reach the yearly goals.

Below is a list of questions that should be ask and answered in order to measure where you are compared to the plan. Sometimes this is not a fun process if the numbers are bad but it has to be done if improvement is going to be made in the business.

Now at every quarterly meeting answer the following questions:

1. What are sales for quarter? _____

2. What is profit for quarter? _____

3. What is sales breakdown: (List each revenue generating area of business) A) _____ B) _____ C) _____ D) _____ E) _____

4. Did we meet our goals?

5. If not why not?

How effective has the marketing program been this quarter? _

How could it be more effective?

What changes need to be made in the marketing program to make it more effective?

What other issues have caused problems this quarter?

How can these issues be resolved?

Are we on track with our goals that were set at beginning of the quarter?

Discuss the goals that need to be put in place for next quarter?

Were emails sent out on time this quarter? (Weekly and monthly)

If they were not sent out on time why not?

What can be done to improve the email marketing?

What are the goals for the next quarter:

Goals: (List sales goals for each separate revenue generating area)
1. _____

2. _____

3. _____

4. _____

5. _____

6. _____

7. _____

8. _____

9. _____

10. _____

Task to be done to reach goals:

Next to each goal put who is responsible for the task. If the goal is not met then the person responsible must tell the other each morning the next week they did not meet that goal and they are working hard so they will reach it this week (NO EXCEPTIONS). If you do not meet goals you are letting down the family)

Monthly Meetings

You will have used your yearly goals to set monthly goals. You will use your gauges to assess your businesses progress each month. When you take these readings you must make sure that they are accurate it. You will use your weekly reviews to assess your monthly performance along with current readings. If your gauges are off then you must look at that department and see why it is not meeting the numbers. You then must ask the employees involved in that department and ask what went wrong and how it can be corrected. Many times they will know and want to correct it. One you have gathered your facts you then must make a correction. You must monitor the corrections to make sure they performing as expected. If everything is on track then take accounting of what is working and why it is working. It is important to know why things are working so you can learn what went right.

Everything you do at these meetings must be written down and kept in a file. This is because in the future if you have a similar problem you can refer back to the pages and see what you did to correct the situation. You must be able to retract your decision at every step.

Questions for Monthly Meeting Review Sheet

1. What were goals for last month?

2. What was actual sales figures?

3. Was company ahead or behind goal?

4. What went right or wrong in past month to cause result?

5. What needs to be addressed for this coming month to ensure goal will be beat this month?

6. What is the goal for this coming month?

7. What steps need to be done to insure beating of goal?

8. What is the plan for month to ensure victory?

9. Has scheduling been done for month?

10. Is any new inventory needed for month?

11. Will you beat this month's goal?

12. Any other business that needs to be addressed:

Weekly Reviews

You will need to review your gauges at the end of each week to see where you are on your journey to success. The sooner you see your gauges are going off then the sooner you can correct it. So when you take the readings follow the same steps you did for the monthly reviews. Make sure everything is written down and that you think through every decision.

Questions for Weekly Review Sheet

1. Are we on track to meet monthly goals?

2. What needs to be done this week to insure success?

3. Who is responsible for doing this?

4. What other issues need to be analyzed this week?

5. Was last week on track to beat monthly goals, if not why?

6. What steps have been taken to correct problems of last week?

Questions for Daily Review

Every day you need to take a moment at the beginning and read your gauges. If there is a problem it is better to catch it early. When you know what is going on your business will run better by just knowing the information because it will make you aware of things like you never dreamed possible.

Daily Review

1. Was yesterday on track to beat week?

2. Can anything be done today to make it a success?

3. What are your major concerns for today?

4. How will you deal with them and who will actually deal with them?

5. What is your goal for today?

6. Will you beat the goal? If not why

Conclusion of Reviews

Like anything in life it will take time to learn to use your gauges and there will be mistakes made if you are trying to use them. But through time like anything you will master the process. The winner is your business in the process because it will follow the road map you completed on its journey to success.

The important thing as we discussed is to write down every step you take in the thought process behind your decisions. Because that way you can learn from mistakes and from successes you make along the way. Running a business is not easy but if you are willing to change to a new way of doing things you will succeed.

As time goes on some of these reviews can be merged into sheets with others because you will be use to the process and your mind will be asking the right question automatically but until then use each form. You may customize it to fit your business but keep the purpose the same. The important thing is to follow the mental map of questioning and finding answers along your journey.

Chapter 14
Marketing and Sales

What is marketing and sales? Why do you need them? Some of you are thinking that this is the easy part because you know how to advertise and your product sells itself. An ad in the newspaper is not a marketing plan.

So what is marketing? Marketing is part of your road map to success. If you have a well developed marketing plan then the road you will travel will be much smoother. A marketing plan must be developed before you open for business. It must be developed so that it runs in unison with the areas of the business. When the marketing plan is developed gauges must be put in place so that the marketing plan's success can be measured and controlled.

What things need to be taken into consideration for a marketing plan? First you must think of your products and list all the people or businesses that would want to purchase them. Make a list under each different customer you may have and then list ways you could market to them. What areas of town do they travel in? What type of magazines or news paper would they read? Can you get there email addresses? Would seminars work to attract these customers? Would outside sales people reach them? Can you reach them through telemarketing? There are many more questions you could ask and you need to ask them. The more questions you can answer about your customers and products the better defined and aimed your marketing plan can be.

Once you have done this you must work with the business office area of your company and figure out an advertising budget that is needed to be successful. You must market to bring in the customers but you can market your business to death. If you over spend you might not be able to pay the rent.

Then you must decide what type of advertising and marketing will best target your customers. These are the people identified in the first series of questions. You then look at what would target them the best and choose the ones that can be done within your budget. The numbers do not lie so don't over spend.

Any marketing choice must be on target to reach the market you choose. If it does not don't do it. No matter how nice the sales person might be. When you can't pay the bill they will no longer be your friend.

Now that you have decided what you will do we must put gauges in place to track the effectiveness of the marketing. When customers do come into your business a way needs to be worked out to find out why they are there and from what source. This does not apply to the ones that buy but to the ones looking as well. What other questions do want to know from your customers and those who make the choice to not do business with you. You have to know this so your marketing plan can be amended to address why these potential customers made a decision not to purchase. The answers might hurt but the old saying "the truth will set free" is true in this case because if you do not listen to this truth it will close YOUR DOORS AND OPEN THE ONE AT YOUR LOCAL BANKRUPTCY COURT AND POSSIBLY TO DIVORCE COURT. Addressing this question will help correct the marketing or product mix that might be the reason for money not finding your cash drawer.

How would find out this information? This information can be gotten from your customers and those that do not buy. Take a few days a week and assign employees to pass out survey forms with the proper questions to get the responses you need to know. In some cases you may even want to talk to them directly. People will usually be very honest with you and appreciated you caring enough to make their shopping experience more enjoyable.

When you get this information you must analyze it and see how you can make your marketing more focused to increase your sales. Why would you want to increase your sales or know why people don't buy? Well as long as the other areas of your business are under control when you have increased sales your profit will go up. Knowing why people don't buy tells you what areas can be improved to increase sales.

I have told you to plan a marketing program and the questions to ask to identify the areas that need to be targeted. But what are the types of marketing you can choose from. You will have every type sales person in the world come in and try to convince you to advertise but they are all not for your business.

Newspaper advertising is a popular form to get your product known. But you must watch it closely because it is expensive and unless you have a large budget it may be ineffective. You must ask yourself will my targeted customer read the paper and will they see my ad. Sunday and Wednesday are the most read papers in most markets.

Radio is another popular form of advertising and once again it is expensive and in order to be effective it must be run often. But if you feel your customers will be listening then it may be a good investment.

TV advertising is a popular form of advertising and in today's market there are many forms. You have the network stations (NBC, FOX, CBS and ABC) they have local news and local programming. Many times you can talk to them and get them to do a story about your business opening. Advertising is expensive but if you have enough money to have your ad on a lot it may be the right fit. The next form of TV is cable. These advertising can be purchased on stations that carry programming your customers will watch. Cable is usually less expensive than network TV. But no matter the type TV advertising you may choose you must track its progress and effectiveness.

Direct mail advertising is a great form of advertising. You can select the zip codes you want to reach and send out advertising mailers. It is a great method if you have a small budget. There are companies that send out mail packages full of coupons if you check around in your area you will find some of them.

Email advertising is a low cost method of marketing. If you have email lists of potential customers you can market directly to them. When you open your business you need to get every email address of every customer you have. Then you can send weekly emails to drive your business. This is the lowest cost of adverting because emailing is free.

Flyers are another low cost form of marketing. You must decide where your customers are and then take flyers around to their office buildings or neighborhoods. This must be done on a regular basis and tracked with your gauges to see which type flyer is working best.

Outside sales force is another marketing method. They are making your products known to the potential customers. A uniformed method of presentation must be designed and implemented. As with all marketing methods you must watch your gauges to make sure they are being effective and how to make them more effective.

Telemarketing is a form of marketing that works well for some business models. It is expensive but if your customers are business owners it works well. You can search the internet and find many different firms. You must track the effectiveness of each telemarketing campaign and use the information to improve it.

Customer referrals are a wonderful way to market your business. Most business owners never ask for referrals from customers and others that come in contact with your business. Simply ask people for others that might like your service or product. A personal referral is the best introduction to do business.

Billboards are another form of marketing. They are excellent for certain type businesses. Just like with all marketing forms you must decide if your customer will be reached by it.

Putting Ads in stores that have public posting areas can be a cost effective way to market. This is advertising on little billboards in other businesses. If you check your local market you will find these companies. You need to figure out where you customer will be and advertise in these places.

Holding a seminar in your customer sales area can be very effective. For certain businesses this is a great way to market. You have to ask can your product or service be sold by holding seminars. Then you have to decide if you can hold a seminar.

Infomercials are another form of marketing. These are long commercials on TV or radio.

Advertising designed as news or an article. This either something mailed to potential customers or run in a newspaper. It is where an advertisement is done to look like a news item or an article. It is an extremely effective form of advertising.

Give away items as marketing. We have all seen this type of marketing in our daily lives. These are pens, cups, note pads, calendars and other items that have your name and number. Watch this type of marketing because if you do not see a return on the marketing then stop participating in it. Store bought pens are cheaper and if you use them you should know your own phone number.

A Web Site as a marketing tool is a great idea. In today's market every business needs a web site. They are inexpensive and should be used in conjunction with the rest of your business. They often take the place of expensive brochures or flyers.

Car Magnets or signs in yards. This is an inexpensive form of marketing that can be very effective. Signs with your name, product or service and phone are great when placed around where your customer will be.

Sponsoring a sports team or scout troop is also an option. This is a way to get your name out and building good will but be careful that you will not make customers mad because you did not sponsor their kids.

Having your name on Menu's around town. This again can be effective if you customers frequent these establishments.

There are many more forms of marketing you can choose from. The most important thing is to monitor the results and make changes as needed. Your marketing plan must be in writing because it is not real unless you put it in writing. Target results must be set and the different areas of your marketing plan must be held accountable.

During the journey to success you will try many different forms of advertising some will work some will not. You must find out why one works and why one does not. Sometimes it is not the form of advertising but the ad itself. Ask yourself does this ad speak to my customer and is it in the correct form to reach them.

Every time you make changes to your marketing plan look at the rest of your structure and see if some other needs to be changed to make the marketing method work more efficient. Everything you do effects all areas of the business so knowing how each area is affected is important. You must watch your gauges when you make changes to your marketing plan. The marketing plan drives your sales and that affects all areas.

For all the fancy marketing terms advertisers use marketing is simply letting people know about your business and getting them to want to do business with you. So whatever you can do to make that happen do it. Because the more people who know about your business the better it will be. Every occupation in the world markets or sales something so don't feel you are above it. Attorneys, Doctors, Accountants, contractors, mechanics, retailers, farmers, panhandlers and any other business you can think of does it. So learn this aspect of your business because it will help make your journey a successful one.

How to handle Sales People

During your journey to success you will be called upon by sales people of all types. From radio ad sales people to product sales people and many other type of people that want your businesses money. It is important to realize that you might need some of these items but you must handle the situation so it is a winning relationship for both. We will go over some tips for dealing with different type of sales people.

Remember the old saying "trust but verify" well when dealing with sales people you must live the saying. Sales people have a slight problem of always looking to the overly positive. Whether they are selling products that will double your business or advertising that will triple your business or at least according to them.

A good general rule is never sign anything until you have thought about it over night. If you use this as a general business rule then when you tell the sales person that you must think about it over night it will be the truth. When you are hearing the sales person spill it is easy to get caught up in the moment and purchase on impulse. So if it is a good idea for your business when the sales person is there it will be a good idea in the morning.

Advertising Sales People:

Advertising is a necessity for your business when used in accordance with your marketing plan. Remember there are many types of advertising that do not take a significant financial investment like calling on potential customers, direct sales force and many more. So every advertiser that calls on you and pitches the one advertising product you can't live without must be compared to your road map. If it does not fit the road map then it is not for your business.

They will tell you how great there advertising medium is so hold them accountable to the numbers they tell you. If the advertising is so good then ask for a free month and for tracking gauges to be put in. If their advertising increases your business to a pre agreed on level then you will enter into an agreement with them. If it does not reach those levels then do not purchase the advertising.

When talking to the sales person ask them what they can do for you as far as things that will benefit you. Often they might have some special program that might help you but if you do not ask you will not know. Ask about opportunities to do sponsorships of programs they might have. Like giving merchandise away on a radio or TV station. That will give your business exposure at a reduced rate. Remember it must fit your road map if it does not do not do it.

Product Sales People:

You will be called on by many product sales people. While you need products to sell to make money over buying can put you out of business. All of the products you buy have to be paid for and anything you buy must fit into you structure and road map. Do not get caught up in the hype.

If the product is something your business needs you then must try to get them at the best deal for your business. Ask the sales person what kind of programs they have to help you put the products into your business. If you don't ask you will never know what they have. Also ask if they can put the merchandise in on consignment. This is where you only pay for what you sell. You can take a count once a week and send the payment for the ones sold. Many companies will do this for you. It will allow you to carry more products and reduce your investment. Remember you only want the product if it fits your road map.

You can also ask for extended terms to pay for your merchandise. If they usually expect payment in 30 days ask for 6 to 9 months if the order is large enough. Then all reorders will be paid in 30 days. This allows you to better cash flow and allows the vendor to record a large sale. They will do it if you show them how it will benefit them.

When dealing with your product sales people you need to address upfront the issue of returns. If someone brings back one of their products you need to establish the exact procedure that will take place to return it to them. If their terms are not acceptable then do not do business with them.

You also need to address how much they will help you in advertising. This is called co-op dollars. Many companies will pay a portion of the advertising if their product is in the ad. This helps absorb the cost of advertising. If done properly with various vendors your entire advertising budget can be covered by others. If you do not ask you do not receive.

If the sales person makes a promise to you then get it in writing. If they want give it to you in writing then they will not honor it and do not do business with them. Everything you need to be in writing not just for you but for the vendor. It cuts down on misunderstanding if everything is in writing.

Business Consultants:

During your journey you might be visited by a business consultant. While they can offer you needed information and tools there are

some out there that are not much better than timeshare sales people. Just as with any other professional you must set expectations
And hold them to it.

I must admonish you that there are groups out in the market place that call themselves consultants that prey on small to medium sized businesses. They will call a business owner or come by and see you. They will set an appointment for a business review or analysis. Then when the business analysis person gets there they will start asking you questions with one goal to make you question yourself. They want you to ask for help when you do they will find out how much money you have and take it. Before you enter into a contract with one of these companies check them out on the internet to see if someone has had problems with them.

Companies such as this give legitimate business consultants a bad name. Consulting will cost money but if it is needed then get it. You should decide what you have to spend and then set up what you expect the consultant to do. If they do not live up to your expectations then do not pay them. Most real consultants want to help your business and will work with you to fit their services in your budget.

Security Companies-Uniform Companies-Cleaning Companies:

If your business needs these services then check around and get quotes from at least 3 companies. Remember to look at their bids not just for price but for the services they provide and if it fits your needs.

Any contract you sign make sure you write in a 30 day cancellation clause. They will tell you many times that is not needed they will just let you out of the contract. When you sign they will not honor their verbal commitment. So get it in writing also make sure there is not any hidden fees.

These services are needed in certain types of businesses. There are many great companies that perform these services but you must make sure your business is safe guarded.

Conclusion:

All of these companies can add value to your company. You must make sure that they are in line with your road map to success. They all want to make money which is fine but you need to make sure your relationship with them profits your business.

You must make sure to do business with these companies in your corporate name so you are not personally responsible for the debt. When you sign always put your corporate position after your name. All the decisions you make in your business must be tied to your overall goal of success. Never make a decision that stands alone.

Success is what waits for you and your business at the end of the journey. So as long as you follow the road map you will be successful. Take pride in yourself every time you make a wise decision and use your road map to do it.

Chapter 15
Keeping Your Business Running

Once you get the doors open and your cash register starts to ring up sales then the work really starts. Think of it like this all of the work you do to open your business is like planning for your trip and stocking your car with everything you will need on the journey but when the journey begins you have to start concentrating on completing the journey. You might be saying my business is now open I have planned it well and have the gauges in place. Why can't I just put it on autopilot for a while? Well you could sit back and relax for a bit. Take time to enjoy life but then you will be living on "Hopium" once again. This is one of the most important journey's you will ever undertake its success or failure will impact your life.

Financial hardship is a leading cause of relationships ending or at least being turned into unpleasant experiences. So why after all of your hard work will you just sit back and wait for the alarm to go off on the autopilot when you are about to hit a bump in the road. But luckily you are just playing with your happiness and financial future bankruptcy court is the result of a fatal crash. If you were really driving or flying a plane it could be death. But for some the thought of having everyone they think of them as a failure is in itself worse than death. But it is your decision.

So after your business gets open and you have all the proper gauges in place it is now time to use them. Because you cannot be at the cash register, out on sales calls, cleaning the warehouse, doing payroll, ordering merchandise, paying taxes, making bank deposits, inspiring your team members and all the other hats a business owner must wear at the same time and do a job that will keep you in business. Every day you must check your gauges that you have installed and when the reading is out of the safe zone you must make a correction.

In the next few pages I am going to address some of the areas and gauges that you might have issues with. Remember every business is different and has some different gauges. So if I do not mention a gauge you feel is important for your business then install it in your business. All businesses will have many gauges the will be the same. You must learn to read the gauge and understand what problem is affecting the gauge. This will come over time but you must make an effort to learn quickly because the quicker you learn the sooner you will be controlling your business.

Profit Gauge

Most people will say they know how to make a profit or they know why they are not making a profit. But this is actually a much deeper topic than you might think. The old adage in business is that if you are not making enough money then you need to raise sales. But even though this does make sense at first glance it actually is assuming a lot and you know what they say about assuming things. This statement is assuming all of you expenses are in line. In other words if you are a retail store it is assuming that your fixed expenses are in line (rent, insurance and ect.) and your variable expenses are in line (cost of product or payroll). Retail businesses should know exactly what their products cost them but many times they forget about shipping cost which should be part of the cost of a good. Restaurants and manufacturing businesses should know what it takes to produce their products. They should know exactly what goes into each product and the cost (They also can't forget shipping). But what if their cooks or assembly line are using more of an ingredient than they are required to and that is running the costs up. Having proper gauges in place to watch your labor costs, product cost, shipping costs, utilities cost, payroll expense, insurance cost, office expense, postage cost, advertising cost, sales cost, promotional cost and any other cost item associated with your business is the only way to truly control your profit.

If you do this properly and use the profit estimation method we discussed you should be able to decide at the beginning of the year how much money you want to make that year. Then plug it into your spread sheet and calculate your goals for the year. Then by watching your gauges you can drive your business toward success and a profit. Because when it goes off course and a gauge is in the danger zone you can take action to correct it now not later. Usually business owners do not realize they are losing money till it is too late but by watching your gauges you will know immediately. What do you do if you think you are losing money?

Well you first look at your gauges see which gauge is not where it should be compared to your estimated goals for each gauge. When you find the gauge that is out of control then study the information going into the gauge to give you that reading. See what is out of control. Then look for ways to bring the reading under control. Use your methods for making a decision we discussed earlier in the book and decide the best way to change it to a positive reading. Then implement the change and monitor its progress.

This must be done hourly in some cases daily at a minimum. It is important to get the gauges back in the proper range so your business is moving toward your profit goal. Simply trying to bring in more money than the problem will not work it is not an efficient way to run your business. If your car is running ineffectively and getting only 1 mile a gallon would it make sense to simply keep putting gas in it? No it would not you would correct whatever was wrong with your engine. Your business is no different it must run at its optimum efficiency.

Expense gauges

The expense gauges have a direct bearing on your profit and its gauge. You must control your expenses if you wish to make a profit. I am sure you have heard people say if my business could only do a million dollars a year I would make big money. But if their expenses were a million and half dollars a year then they would be in trouble. That is why you must run your business on percentages that way the number makes sense immediately. You do not have to wonder how that number stands in when compared to your revenue or profit. When you figure your goals for the year in a percentage form and your revenue increases or decreases the goal still holds true.

When an expense gauge starts to go into the danger area you must once again follow the steps to make a decision. Then implement your decision and continue to monitor it. When trying to correct the problem you may have to make several changes before you find the right combination. But remember to keep everything in a written form so you can study the results of each change and make a better decision the next time around.

It will amaze you when you start studying your expenses and controlling them how much money you can change from expenses to profit. Because every dime you save is money you earn. From watching the paper that is wasted in your business to saving energy it all adds up to more profit. Don't ever take anything for granted when trying to cut expenses even when you don't think you can cut any more money you more than likely can cut more. Make saving money a topic for your company meetings. Maybe give an award for ideas to save money for the company. Because the easiest way to increase profit is to cut expenses and making more money is the goal.

When cutting expenses though make sure you distinguish between cutting expenses and cutting fuel to grow sales. Cutting effective advertising or inventory could cost you in the long run. Because you have gauges on every aspect of your business you will know if a form of advertising is effective or what inventory level is the best.

Work Force Gauges

How many workers do you need? This is a question that will be a constant issue within your business if you are watching your gauges. You want enough workers to handle the business effectively but not too many to cause your payroll gauge to go into the danger zone. You must also address how to pay your work force. What type of benefits should you offer? All of these issues must have separate gauges so you can see the effect on your business.

Let's look first at how do you pay your work force? Some people think a straight hourly wage is the best and holds down your cost. But is a person that gets paid the same whether they work hard or not so hard still do the work you need? Every position should be paid in some sort of performance based scale. From the office workers to your salespeople it will work. You can pay an hourly wage but put a bonus on their pay plan if they hold down costs and your company hits its profit goals. This will cause everyone to work harder and care about what happens at your company.

The sales staff is easy to put on a performance base plan they should be on commission. In my opinion a sales staff should have a small base pay with the rest of their income coming from their performance. You might find many of your sales staff saying they would rather be on salary because they like stability. If this happens you have hired the wrong people for that position. A sales person should be driven to sale and want to be rewarded for their hard work. One problem that happens many times when a salesperson really performs and starts making big money the owner of the business thinks the salesperson is being paid too much. Business owners have been known to get rid of a highly paid salesperson and replace with one on a salary or a lower commission rate only to find that they are making less because of lower sales. So make sure your pay structure works with your overall business structure and road map you created if the structure works then be happy that your sales people make lots of money that means you are doing your job. You will also be making lots of money if you are watching your gauges.

In order to set up a performance based pay scale for non sales positions you will have to isolate each position in your business structure then identify which gauges that position affects. These are the gauges that this position will be paid a bonus on improving performance of the gauge. Say they are part of a cleaning crew and you usually use $1,000 in cleaning supplies each quarter. Then maybe set that as your bench mark and then set out to improve it. If your cleaning crew saves $200 the next quart then give them a $100 bonus. You can divide the bonus by the number of workers then this is their bonus. If there are other gauges that apply this position then add that gauge to the mix and then watch your company's performance improve. Your goal is to make every position in the company responsible for their gauges.

Now how many employees do you need to run efficient? You must study your gauges and see what level of work force lets that gauge work the best. You want enough labor to take care of business but not enough to have them standing around. The fewer people that can do the job that are needed the better it is for everyone. Your company can afford to pay more money in salaries and supply better benefits. You will have to watch this gauge constantly to see if more help is needed or if the work force must be trimmed. What type of benefits do you need to supply for your employees? Many business owners feel this is an expense they cannot afford. But your employees are an important part of your business structure and you should try to give them the benefits they need. Does this mean pay for everything? No, but as a group you can get a better deal with an insurance carrier. You can offer it and have them pay all of it or a part of it. There are many sources for insurance for your company employees. You can go to an insurance broker or direct to the insurance company to get quotes. Most states have insurance packages for small business owners and employees. This coverage is usually has a limit of $25,000 or $50,000 a year coverage but this is good coverage. It lets your employees feel good that you care enough to protect them and their families. So make sure you check with your state for any insurance coverage that may be available.

Insurance is not the only benefit that you can provide. You can find a credit union in your area and sign up for your employees to be able to join. You can give company cards to a discount shopping club as a benefit (Sam's, Costco and many others).

But you must make sure your company structure can afford to provide the benefits you choose to pay for. Because the pay check you give your employees will not last if you over extend your business. So make sure the revenue is there before going out and getting a package of benefits you cannot afford to pay for. Benefits are important to give to your work force but only when your business structure can handle it. If you cannot afford it then still make it available and have options for them.

How to hold Your Company meetings

One of the most valuable tools available to you as a business owner is the company meeting. Most business owners only have a meeting when something is wrong and they become feared. But you should have a regular meeting at least once a month. Once a week is difficult with the daily work load but if you can truly hold one once a week it will bring returns to your company.

A company meeting is not a time to complain about the performance of the company. Because you choose the work force for the positions you created in your business structure. You read your gauges on a daily basis and make adjustments to each area of your company. So if the work force is the problem is not really your fault. So go into the bathroom and look in the mirror. Take a good look and then scream at the person that is at fault for the condition of your company.

If a position is not being run right by the person that fills the position then work with that person and get improvement. If improvement does not come then switch the person for that position because not to do so is not to do your job. Make sure this time you do a better job of choosing the person for the position. But a company meeting is not the time to tell everyone that you have not been a good job directing them.

A company meeting should be used to direct your company toward the goals that have you set. The meeting should start on a review of all the goals that have been met or projects finished since the last meeting. If a position has done an outstanding job for the company honor the person that fills that position. Then review the challenges that were overcome since last meeting. If there was some corrections that were needed to make your goals and they met them then go over the positive effect of their work. Then review the goals that were not met (Don't complain just state facts) and ask for suggestions on how the company can make sure these goals at met. Getting your work force involved in solving problems makes them feel part of the solution.

Then go over the goals for the current period and lay out your plan for reaching the goal. If you want to offer a special incentive to the company work force if the goal is met then offer it here. Don't forget to pass out copies of the goals for the period you are talking about. If you want to put a signature section at the bottom and ask everyone in the company that will work to make this goal reality to sign. Then have them turn it back in this will have mentally make a commitment to this goal.

Ask for any questions from the company and then thank them for all of their hard work. Wish them well and tell them your door is always open. Just like in a marriage communication is imperative for success and it must be two way not just complaining. If a marriage has no communication or a business owner does not communicate with their workers both will end up in court. One will be divorce court the other is bankruptcy court. Often business failure leads to a person visiting both so communicate it is to your benefit.

Don't forget like everything in your business your company meeting must be gauged and monitored. This gauge will be in the improved moral and performance of your workers after a meeting.

If you see no improvement try changing up the meeting but keep having them once you have mastered them your business will improve through them.

When to Terminate a Worker one of the toughest things for most people to do is to terminate an employee. But in order to keep your business going you must do this well. If you hire properly you will have to do it less but you will still have to terminate people. This should not be hard to do because before you get to this point you will have worked hard to change their behavior.

When your gauges show that a position in your company is not being run right you will work with that person to improve. You will meet with them and have them give their input to what the problem is with the position. A road map will be put together for them to follow to improve. If improvement is not seen then you will meet with them and try to find out what is wrong. If improvement is not seen and your gauge is in danger of damaging the performance of the company then the position must be refilled.

When you make this decision you need to make sure that you make sure you follow the laws in your state for terminating an employee. Then schedule a meeting and sit down in private with the employee. Make sure you review the work that has been done to try to get them to improve and that no improvement has been seen. Then tell them this position is not for them and that you appreciate their time with the company. Make sure you get all keys or passwords for their computer (You may want to get these before you fire them). If you can get their last paycheck and have it for them when you terminate their relationship with your company this is a nice jester it also leaves no reason for them to come back to your business. Terminated employees cause problems by talking to still employed people so limiting their contact with employees is a good idea.

Make sure you save your file with the problems with that position and the work you did trying to improve their performance. If violating company rules or stealing is involved be sure to document all prove of such behavior. If they file with unemployment to draw unemployment you will have an opportunity to dispute them getting it.

Watching your gauges will make controlling your employees performance much easier than simply watching them work every once in a while. The results of their work will show in your gauges. If an employee is not trying to improve then they do not care about your company so do not feel remorse for giving them the freedom to find a job they like.

Conclusion

We have reviewed some gauges that will be used in your business and some suggestions on using them. But this is your business so if you want to change the gauges or edit some other facet of your business then do so but make sure you are doing it to make your business more effective and not to do less work. Your success depends on knowing what is happening in your business. Success is the reason you are setting out on this journey. You may not want to make a million dollars a year so you may say why should I know everything that happens in my business? Well you need to know what goes on in your business by using gauges because you might want to be in business at the end of the month.

Chapter 16
Go Start Your Journey

Well you have made it to the end of this book. You are ready to start using the decision making methods we went over and decide on a business to open or decide not to open a business. Because it is better not to open a business if you will not do the work that is necessary to set your business up right. If you will do the work necessary to choose a business and plan your road map you can be successful on your journey.

Please take time when choosing what business to go into because it is a big decision. If you are having difficulty in choosing a business you may visit the SBA web site and review some of the businesses we have listed there. These are business plans that take just a little money to open and include a DVD that shows a step by step process to open that type business.

This is your decision so don't let anyone else tell you what you should do with this journey you have chosen. This must be a business you believe in and feel you can build the structure and road map necessary for success.

Don't jump into anything without thinking and reasoning each decision. I want you to understand the concepts we have talk about in this book because they will help you succeed on your journey. People all over the country dream of owning a business but just don't know how to do it. My goal with this book is to show you how to make your dreams reality. Knowledge is power so gather as much knowledge as possible before you start your journey.

The American dream is possible and you deserve to be successful. No matter what size of business you dream of having it is possible. Don't let anyone tell you that success is for others or it is not your time. Time is what you make of it and if you build a successful business structure and a good road map the journey to success will be yours. It does not take superior intelligence to build a successful business but the ability to follow your road map. You can be the master of your own destiny.

So if you are ready to start your journey take the rest of the day off and then first thing in the morning start work on designing the road map for your journey to success. No one will do it for you so if you want to own a business and have it become successful make tomorrow morning the first day of your journey to success.

www.ingramcontent.com/pod-product-compliance
Lightning Source LLC
Chambersburg PA
CBHW061513180526
45171CB00001B/164